As It Should Be

Tales of Old Florida

The Land, The People, The Times

By Lance A. Edwards

Dedication

This book is dedicated to the Florida women in my life:

Mom (Judy Porter Edwards Hopkins), who made it all possible – literally and figuratively; for over half a century, she's my unwavering support in my sea journey of life (including the meticulous editing of this manuscript – any errors are mine);

Nana (Theodora Viola "Pat" Edwards Safford), who embodied the romance of the state. Even as a transplanted Yankee, she did it better than most native Floridians;

And to my wife, Kim Fox Edwards, who brought joy into my life; and enabled me to experience Old Florida again, thirty-five years after I embarked on my journey away from home.

Table of Contents

Preface

This book is fifty years in the making. And although I've previously written a best-selling book for commercial purposes, this book was written for purely personal reasons. I expect it to be read by only a few people (and likely enjoyed by even fewer).

This is the story of Old Florida told by an old Floridian; recounted in vignettes of the people, the land, and the times. If I've done my job properly, you'll laugh and cry with the tales of this special place and these special people during the three-decade span of the 1960's thru the 1980's (and actually before; reaching all the way back to frontier Florida in 1848). My family was there the entire time and I share Old Florida thru my family's lens.

In the process of researching this book, I visited numerous libraries, cemeteries, and museums. Mom (Judy Porter Edwards Hopkins) was there with me for many of those trips. I've connected the dots to find the common thread of the Real Floridians – self-made people who bet it all; who, thru their actions, revealed the true American spirit which is found across the entire nation and in so many other families just like mine.

Unfortunately, most of the people are now gone; the times have passed, and the land is being permanently changed. Hence my reason for capturing it all to paper before I (and my memory) become part of that same past.

What to Expect

Not to give away the plot line (so to speak) but within the confines of this book you'll learn about the fortunes made from citrus and cattle – wild resources left behind by sixteenth century Spanish explorers.   You'll discover the wealth in ancient dead fish; transformed over millions of years into phosphate. You'll also learn about a live fish: Snook. You'll laugh at the Hoboken canoers, and the exploits and ingenuity of the Robalo Club members. You'll follow the die-hard Florida Gator fans thru disappointment after disappointment, finally to be redeemed after the return of their Football Messiah.

You'll visit locations varying between orange groves and mangroves; spring water to salt water; pancake flat prairies to prehistoric ridge lines. You'll experience the few remaining places that most humans don't even know exist and are rarely disturbed. You'll walk the ancient Indian mounds. You'll wade back into time thru the eons and walk the same locations the prehistoric animals wandered, leaving their fossil evidence behind.   And, in the process, you'll discover, like me, that everything is connected. Obvious in hindsight, it's rarely apparent in the moment.

You'll witness the wonderment of nature, untarnished by human contact: the tranquility of a mangrove canopy over a hidden creek; pine islands which pop up like an oasis on the flat prairie; the intelligence of porpoises who corral mullet as a team before batting them high into the air with their tails; the gentleness of a manatee as it rolls on its back for a belly rub, and the violent power of a Snook taking the bait. These are just a few of the *As It Should Be* experiences I'll attempt to paint into words.

Manatee In the Mangroves

At the same time, you'll experience the power of Mother Nature to likewise "hike her skirt and kick your butt," as Dad used to say. Imagine Christmas Eve and the temperature outside is plummeting below freezing and the question on everyone's mind in citrus country is, "Forget the oranges. Will the orange trees survive?" (A relevant financial question for the Citrus Capitol of the World and the Edwards clan, three-generation citrus people.)

Together, we'll "batten down the hatches" with the approach of each hurricane as Mother Nature yet again takes her best shot. And you'll also step thru the stench of dead and decaying fish and mammals, brought about by man's ignorance and arrogance in water management. Along the way, there will even be some murder, followed by instant vigilante street justice against the accused.

I'll cover broad topics ranging from the best fish, the best gun, the best shot, the best boat, the best beach, the best food, the best beer, the best bourbon, to the best bar. And since no story would be complete without religion, I'll throw in some college football, leading to... the best team.

Of course, there are the people - those self-made resilient and God-fearing people with God-given human foibles and fears who nevertheless steadfastly saw their way through; the men who kept the wolves from the door; the even-stronger women who placed all of their trust in their men. And, in too many cases, had to keep the wolves away on their own, when their men failed them.

Good people - *As It Should Be* people - who you knew you could trust. You did business on a hand shake. Many of them were described as *"fish corks,"* meaning "You can push him down but he'll pop right back up." Just like the irreverent men I portray here, I am one of their irreverent disciples. In fact, if anyone were to try coming after one of us, they'd have to deal with all of us. It was part of The Code. There will be some mildly coarse language but, knowing that Mom will be proofreading this, rest assured that this is the PG version of the R-rated life experience.

I'm an engineer by training. And as an engineer, I'm no expert on the human condition, but I was a scientific observer of the greatest minds on successful living. If you ever saw the TV show, Rockford Files, or you've read any of the Travis McGee novels by John D. MacDonald, you can perhaps gain an insight to just some of the strong and interesting characters of this story, self-made men and women. In fact, one of the early working titles for this book was, "I Knew the Real Travis McGees." However, that title would have belittled the scope of this story (and undoubtedly brought down a pack of lawyers) so I stuck with the natural title, *As It Should Be.*

"As It Should Be" was a favorite saying of my father, Arthur Tillis Edwards III, or A.T. (Dad to me). As you can imagine, Dad is at the center of many of my childhood experiences – experiences that most twelve-year-olds don't get to witness till late adulthood, if ever. As he once said to me, as we sat at his private table at the El Greco Bar, in Lakeland, Florida, celebrating my completion of graduate school, "Son, you may have a Master's degree from Notre Dame but you got your real education here." As I grew into adulthood, I came to discover he was right. In fact, what I learned growing up in Old Florida would ultimately serve me from Houston to Tokyo; from the streets to the board room.

But I'm getting ahead of my story.

Let's get back to *As It Should Be.*

As It Should Be

As It Should Be captures the longing for a better time, the best of times; a craving for and recognition of proper behaviors, proper attitudes, proper respect. It represents a code of what's right and what's wrong and when it's proper to do what's wrong in order to make things right again. It's romantic. It's spiritual. It's a philosophy. It transcends what can be seen and, in fact, it can't be seen – only experienced after a couple decades of indoctrination and orientation.

In addition, I've discovered it's not just a Southern thing or even an American thing. In Japan, the ancient Samurai called it *bushida* – their code for a life of honor and duty. It's probably why there's such a strong sense of duty and honor, and respect, for all things military amongst Old Floridians.

The *As It Should Be* code is demonstrated in many ways by Old Floridians. For example, it can be as simple as the raising of a glass between lifelong friends at sunset over the Gulf; the shared and silent appreciation for all things good – and recognition that at that precise moment, all is well within the universe. All communicated with no spoken words other than *"As It Should Be."*

It can be manifested amongst 50,000 screaming and crazy fans at a Florida Gators football game in Jacksonville when our beloved Gators beat the arch-rival Georgia Bulldogs. After the shouting and screaming finally subsides, the appropriate response would be, *"As It Should Be!"*

When we read on Facebook how a single mother held off a man attempting to hijack her car with her child in the backseat – using her concealed 45 pistol, the immediate response and universal thought amongst Old Floridians is, *"As It Should Be."*

When our veterans or active military walk thru an airport in formation, and the rushed travelers stop to applaud them in unison, that's an *As It Should Be* moment. When we stand in awe of the power of the Blue Angels on a low-pass fly-by, and instantly reflect of all things great and powerful with America, that's an *As It Should Be* moment. I will reveal more within the chapters to come.

The vignettes and stories I share here are intended to resonate with those of us who understand and miss Old Florida. And if I really stretch my writing skills, I'll even appeal to those who have never personally experienced Old Florida, or knew of its experience prior to this publication. At least, you'll hopefully be able to recall your own simpler times and tougher people – no matter the geographic location.

What is Old Florida?

For those of us raised in Florida, we know of Old Florida but if you're not familiar with this saying, then I should help define it. You really can't appreciate the stories without the basis of this reference point.

Old Florida is more than a geographic location. It's a mindset, a feeling, a time of strong family bonds and behaviors and traditions of respect, self-reliance, and individual fortitude. It's the place where you say "Yes sir" and "Yes ma'am," no matter your age. Old Florida finds its heritage in the Florida Cracker families who scratched out a living in the Florida scrub (the piney woods and wild prairies of Central Florida), despite all odds.

Old Florida is indeed as much the land as it is the people. It is the unspoiled native Florida land in its ultimate beauty – which is truly loved by native Floridians.

What Old Florida is NOT is Disney World or high-rise condos on the beach or the bulldozing of the orange groves for trailer parks and box homes which strips the state of its clean water and threatens its very existence.

It is not my intent to get on my conservatory soap box but I do believe Old Florida has been traded for a New and Unimproved Florida. It's a fine line, but to me, Old Florida is the now gone, but individually-owned tourist stands on the side of the highway, where you could buy a bag of oranges and pet an alligator; citrus stands owned and operated by Mom and Pop, who were simply another version of the Florida Cracker Mom and Pop who survived the Florida scrub.

Old Florida Souvenir and Citrus Stand

Old Florida was attractions like Silver Springs where you could experience Florida's natural beauty while cruising in a glass-bottomed boat. Or Gatorland on Highway 27 where you could see an alligator ride a unicycle – or something like that. Or Six Gun Territory where, as a boy, you could see an actual gun fight played out on the streets. The common thread of these attractions was the fact that they were each family owned – Mom and Pop Floridians carving out their living. That Old Florida was basically killed by Disney and the other corporations who came to harvest, in mass, the state's land and beauty.

As a birthday gift to myself a couple years ago, my wife, Kim, and I visited Silver Springs on the way to a Gators football game weekend. Yes, Silver Springs, the attraction, still exists – but barely. At that time, the attraction had been abandoned by its private owners, due to its impossible fiscal performance, and the state had taken it over. The buildings were shuttered and dilapidated. The glass-bottom boats were still running but the crowds were thin. And the springs were spewing their tens of thousands of gallons of water per minute - or hour (I can't remember) - but as I enjoyed the beauty, I couldn't help but think, "How soon til these springs run dry?" After all, it's happened all over the state.

In July 1969, when I was seven, our family spent a one-month summer vacation on Longboat Key – a barrier island on the West coast of the state. The cottages were appropriately named, White Sands Cottages. The place was beautiful; I recall the month and date (July 20, 1969) because Mom held me in front of an old black and white TV set, with rabbit ears, to witness Neil Armstrong taking man's first step on the moon. I couldn't appreciate it at the time but I remember that moment to this day. Roll the clock forward fifty years and now, much of that Old Florida is gone, replaced by high rise condos and timeshares – designed to stuff more people into the same square feet of land.

Today, Kim and I split our time between our new Old Florida beach home on Palm Island in Southwest Florida and our Houston home, where my business is headquartered. I'll end this section on Old Florida by using the story of our moving back to Florida as an explanation of what Old Florida means – at least to me.

Returning to Old Florida

In October 2016, Kim and I were married. I was a widower and Kim was divorced when we met (I should say reconnected in January 2014) after thirty-five years. You see, Kim (Fox) and I have known each other since the first grade. We were both raised in Lakeland, Florida – the former Citrus Capitol of the World – in Central Florida. We not only met in the first grade but we graduated high school together at Lakeland Senior High School in 1979. We literally grew up together - as friends.

Following high school graduation, we embarked on our own lives: college, marriage, family, careers, travel around the world. I ended up living in Houston. Kim lived all over for the next 30 years following college. In 2014, at fifty-something years old (Kim will kill me for writing this), our lives would intersect again.

My wife had died a few years prior; my daughter, Stephanie, was grown and on her own. I was alone in Houston running my business, having survived the Great Recession. Kim had divorced, was working as a loan officer and had moved back to Florida – home. I was having the same thoughts – returning to Old Florida to be back around family and old friends.

While visiting Mom in Lakeland for Thanksgiving in 2013, I visited my first open house as my early exploratory steps into a possible move back to Florida. The house was not for me, but on the kitchen countertop there was a mortgage flyer and, at the bottom, it had a picture and name of the loan officer, Kim Fox. My immediate response to the realtor was, "I know her. I went to school with her."

Thanks to Facebook, I was able to find and reconnect with Kim (Kim claims I stalked her on Facebook). Two months later (January 2014) on a return trip to Lakeland, I asked Kim to have dinner with me. We didn't call it a date but it was our first date - ever. We dined at the Bonefish Grill.

Despite the fact that we had not seen or spoken or thought of the other for thirty-five years, it was like we had seen each other the day before. There was instant chemistry (or maybe I should say fifty years of old chemistry reignited). It was like coming home – to Old Florida; all the same values, common friends, likes and dislikes catalyzed the bond. And we've been together ever since that reconnection dinner.

We were married on the beach in Florida – at a place called Palm Island; a barrier island on the Southwest Gulf Coast of Florida. And this is where the move back to Old Florida and the writing of this book begins…

Lance and Kim's Wedding. Palm Island, 2016
Bride Side: Kevin Fox, Keith Fox, Ray Fox, Nell Fox (l-r)
Groom Side: Stephanie Edwards, Judy Edwards Hopkins, Duane Hopkins, Brian Edwards (l-r)

Palm Island

We chose Palm Island for the wedding because Kim's parents had owned a condo there for twenty years and it was a special place for Kim and her family (plus Kim's first marriage was there and I think we got a repeat-buyer discount). I didn't know the place existed until Kim introduced it to me.

Initially, I didn't like it – for a number of reasons. First of all, the only way to get on the island is by ferry and it's $50 per round trip – the one-way trip is exactly four minutes, covering a water distance of maybe two hundred yards from island to mainland. It's a pricy trip. Then, once you're on the island, you can't drive your car on the island; you park your car and everyone gets around in rented golf carts (more expense).

There's only one restaurant on the island and it doesn't serve breakfast. And there's just one bar (in the restaurant) that closes at 10:00 pm because that's when the ferry shuts down for the night. Bottom line, when you're on Palm Island, you're isolated.

But here's the brilliance and beauty of the place which I finally came to realize. Palm Island is Old Florida, protected. Here's how fate not only brought Kim and me back home but led to this book finally being written.

Shortly after we were married, Kim and I were toying around with the idea of buying Kim's parents' condo on Palm Island. Kim wanted to have a place she called her own and I wanted to provide that for her. On a visit there, and discussing the idea with her parents, I asked Kim, "Instead of a condo, why don't we buy a house?" That question led to the purchase of our house on Palm Island in March 2017 – five months after being married.

It was during the house purchase that I came to realize the brilliance of Palm Island and its developer, Dean Beckstead. Unlike other developers who look to harvest the land at its expense, Palm Island was developed not only as a commercial venture but to preserve Old Florida. And that realization was when I came to quickly appreciate and love the place.

The ferry which I originally hated due to the expense; it keeps the island isolated and blocks the hordes of beach goers, the scourge of too many Florida beaches. The automobile restriction which I initially found so inconvenient; that keeps things simple and at a speed that can't exceed ten miles per hour while preserving the pristine nature of the island with no asphalt but instead, shell roads. But that's not all. Even the architecture is restricted.

I'm probably the only prospective owner who actually read the entire Development Declarations from 1983 but it declares that the island is deed restricted such that no condo is more than two stories tall and all houses must comply to "Old Florida" architectural style. That's right, it's a requirement to build. Dean had literally written that in.

And so, today, you have on Palm Island an Old Florida hideaway, land-locked by geography and time-locked thru its Old Florida deed restrictions. Sadly, we lost Dean in April 2018; before I could tell him what a masterful – and unique – job he had achieved with his creation.

Hence, my reconnecting with Kim, my middle-age reflection over life and my introduction to Palm Island led to this book. As Dad would say, "That's *As It Should Be.*"

Lance, Kim and Riley on Palm Island

Lance Edwards
Palm Island, Florida
January 2019

The Back Story

The Smithsonian Museum in Washington D.C. maintains separate and very large storage centers outside of Washington to house all of the items that are not on display. I understand the reasoning now. In writing a history book, it is an unending process of discovery. There's always something else. It becomes the writer's choice of how deep (or not) to go.

Fortunately, we live in a digital age and we are not limited to the confines of this book. So, I created a website, akin to the Smithsonian's warehouse of additional archives where you can dive deeper into topics of interest. You can see unpublished photos, hear oral histories from the actual people or see a video synopsis.

At the end of each chapter, you'll see a section like this labeled "The Back Story" where you can further enjoy a multimedia experience with regards to that chapter.

For additional background information, audio and video interviews and/or the unpublished photos for this chapter, visit:

BONUS: The Back Story - Preface
http://www.AISBbook.com/Preface

Chapter 1

Stilt Cabin at Marker #63

In 1965, Dad's good friend, Bobby Fore, without any prompting or explanation whatsoever, said, "Arthur, give me a hundred dollars." Without a "What for?" or any hesitation, Dad handed Bobby the hundred. And in that moment was launched a string of characters and life experiences whose telling could easily fill this entire book. That one hundred dollars was Dad's initiation fee into the Robalo Club.

Robalo

The Robalo Club was a private group of Lakeland men who had a common interest – the pursuit of Robalo, more commonly known in Florida as Snook; arguably the greatest fish ever made. Snook is uniquely Floridian because other than the Southern reaches of Texas, you cannot find Snook in the United States. It requires the subtropical waters of Florida. It flourishes on both coasts of the state, from the Southern Everglades northward to Tampa Bay.

The mere mention of the name elicits emotion from Old Florida fishermen like few other fish; actually none that I can think of. Snook draws its charisma from its demeanor, its hiding places, its fighting capability and its taste. As far as I'm concerned, no fish tastes better – especially one you've successfully wrestled into the boat after a desperate fight for survival.

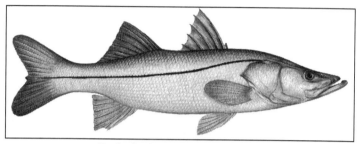

Robalo (Common Snook)

Snook lurk in the most fishiest of places, places that are totally unique to Florida. Snook are an aggressive species who prefer to ambush bait fish from hidden spaces. They especially love to lurk amongst mangrove roots where they can hide in the shade, awaiting their next meal to come along. You can likewise find them under docks and piers, again under the cover of shade.

Snook especially like strong moving tides so that the moving water brings the bait to the Snook. You could say they are basically lazy creatures who jump into action once the topic of food, or sex, comes about (I suppose women could say the same of most men). However, once they are presented a bait, Snook jump into action like few other gamefish. Pound-for-pound, there is no better fighter, because they are strong and smart.

Snook seem to have an inbred sense of exactly how to drag your thin fish line around a barnacled pier or mangrove root. But in the process, he's likely to first give you a dance on the water as he works to shake the hook. I swear nothing gets a fisherman more excited than the sight of a Snook violently taking the bait and the pursuing fight.

And it's the Snook's affinity for mangroves, piers and moving water that contributes to the fish's popularity with Old Floridians. You catch them in "fishy-looking" places. In fact, it's common to refer to a patch of water as "Snooky-looking."

It's simply not the same as fishing for bass or speckled perch or snapper. There's not the same excitement in the hunt, the location, the anticipation of an attack and the fight. Snook carry amongst Old Floridian fishermen a special reverence. It's like the old E.F. Hutton commercials, "When E.F. Hutton talks, people listen." Well, you start telling a Snook story in any bar in Old Florida and you'll silence the room and draw a crowd. The fish is that mystical, that alluring, that mysterious.

It was this Old Floridian affinity for Snook that led to the creation of the Robalo Club. And it was the Snook's affinity for mangroves that led Dad, my brother Brian and me, and countless friends since, to the Ten Thousand Islands of the Everglades…

The Ten Thousand Islands

When most people think of the Everglades, they think of the "river of grass" description made popular by Marjorie Stoneman Douglas' book of the same title. It's a massive land mass situated in South Florida and now (thank God) protected as a natural park (not that it isn't dying anyway but that will come later).

What most people are not aware of is the Western portion of the Everglades is known as the Ten Thousand Islands. And this is where my story takes place.

In contrast to the "river of grass" portion of the Everglades where acres and acres of sawgrass flats probably come to mind, the Ten Thousand Islands is a collection of "ten thousand" mangrove jungle islands separated by bays and intertwining creeks, and bordered on the West by the Gulf of Mexico. Other than the last bastion of civilization at Chokoloskee (population 349) on the Northern end of the Ten Thousand Islands, there are no human inhabitants between Chokoloskee and Flamingo to the South; probably a four to five-hour boat trip at full throttle. Ten Thousand Islands is one of the few no-man lands left in the United States. At least when you're there, that's what you feel like.

It's such an intertwining maze of creeks and bays, it's remarkably easy to get yourself lost and not be able to find your way out. Imagine a Florida version of the African Queen but in a maze of twisting creeks and bays, surrounded by mangrove jungles.

GPS doesn't even help in navigation because GPS cannot warn you of the sand bars which can beach you and the oyster bars which can knock a blade off your prop, leaving you stranded until the next human being (might) come by via boat.

The Ten Thousand Islands (we called them the Glades) is home to not only Snook but redfish, trout, tarpon, fourteen-foot alligators, snakes of all types and venoms, docile manatees, prehistoric-looking sawfish, intelligent and playful porpoises, nesting osprey and bald eagles, robber raccoons and even the rare Florida panther. But its largest inhabitant population is that of the common mosquito; mosquitoes so thick and so potent that the mere buzzing sound of them around your head can drive a man crazy. And their bites and welts on your neck, arms and legs can cause a man to scratch his bloody hide off, in a futile effort to halt the itch.

It's a spooky and wonderful place. And, as you might be able to tell, it's also a place that can make your visit a living hell if you don't respect it and don't know or pay attention to what you're doing.

Unbeknownst to Dad, this is the location where the Robalo Club had chosen to erect a fishing cabin, right dab in the middle of the mangroves and the mosquitoes – a one-hour boat ride due South from Chokoloskee. And once Dad learned of this plan, that's when he told his friend, Bobby…

Give Me My Money Back

Dad's one previous experience with the Glades had been more likely described as a "living hell." You see, to most camping visitors to the Ten Thousand Islands, your experience is like this…

You launch from Chokoloskee in your boat by motor – or canoe. (If you really want the hellish tour, use a canoe.) You traverse the bays, rivers and creeks surrounded by nothing but tropical mangrove jungle; that's actually the beautiful part. But depending on the season, you'll be savaged by the sun, the heat and the bugs. All of which is controllable thanks to the miracles of technology: bimini tops for your boat, cooler chests of ice, and bug repellant of every shape and size, including battery-operated devices. (By the way, the best Everglades-tested and proven bug repellant is Avon's

Skin So Soft. That's right, skin cream - drives the flying insects crazy.)

While we're on the topic of bugs, I should emphasize that we're not talking about your everyday home-variety mosquito. These are ferocious, blood sucking critters; competing with a jillion other mosquitoes for your blood. And if that's not enough, there's also the deer fly. A deer fly looks like a house fly except it's yellow instead of gray. And there's one other important distinction from the house fly, it bites – HARD. And a deer fly can actually bite thru a man's socks and his Levi's! I'm not embellishing here; these guys are nasty. Which is why you have to wear long pants and long sleeves in the Glades – to thwart off the sun and the bugs. So while you're enjoying your time in Sunny Florida, you do so wrapped in clothes. Forget shorts and t-shirts. No, no, no, that's the super hellish tour – saved for the unknowing. I'll share the details of that version later.

That's just the day-time description of your Ten Thousand Islands camping tour. At night, it can become downright maddening. First, you have a choice of elaborate campsites. One choice is a chickee; a chickee is a man-made standalone dock, attached to no land - probably fifty to one hundred yards from the nearest mangrove. Built by the park service, they feature a dock with a surface area large enough to pitch a tent, a place to tie up your boat, a roof and a porta-john. Of course, there's no electricity; the closest chickee to Chokoloskee is a one-hour boat trip – on a full plane.

Ten Thousand Islands Chickee – Mangroves in Background

Your second choice is even more elaborate and saved for the real survivalist types: a land-based campsite amidst the mangroves. Also constructed by the Park Service (with a chain saw), the rangers cut back a small portion of mangroves - about the size of your living room. They may throw in a picnic table and grill for all the comforts of home but it's a trap. This ain't home and this ain't no picnic. You see, the real advantage of the mangrove camp is that you have a front row seat – correction, you are seated on the fifty yard line (on the field) of the super bowl of mosquito savagery. You have landed in their territory. If mosquitoes could tote chain saws, there'd be a thousand of these man-traps laid out for unsuspecting campers across the Ten Thousand Islands.

If you choose the mangrove camp option, be prepared for a full evening of an uninterrupted symphony of mosquitoes buzzing around your tent and head. They're relentless. Now, they will let up with sunrise, but by that time you're so exhausted from lack of sleep and scratching that you can't even really enjoy the reprieve. And, by the way, you're sopping wet, laying in your own sweat because the temperature only drops to eighty-five degrees at night. So, you're tired, stinky, wet and have a full day of heat and more bugs to look forward to. Yea, that's a good time.

That pretty much describes Dad's first experience to the Ten Thousand Islands and why he demanded his money back from Bobby. It wasn't the hundred dollars that mattered; it was the idea that, as a new member of the Robalo Club, he had committed himself to returning to his first hellish experience. "Nope," Bobby said. "You don't get your money back. You're in."

The Robalo Club

Perhaps never before has there been assembled a more charismatic, entertaining, irreverent group of men as the members of the Robalo Club. Respected in business circles, they became the Old Boy network once they were unleashed from the constraints of cosmopolitan Lakeland. Remember the Rat Pack of Frank Sinatra, Dean Martin, Sammy Davis Jr, and Peter Lawford? Recall the image of each of them with a cigarette in one hand, bourbon in another, tux, laughing, shooting pool. Now visualize the same crew on boats in the Ten Thousand Islands: a redneck Rat Pack. That was the Robalo Club.

Not one of these members could be termed a survivalist. Not one of them, in their wildest dreams, was interested in camping in the Glades – whether it was the chickee option or the mangrove option. But they each were religiously interested in pursuing Robalo (Snook) wherever they could be found. And the Glades would become their place of worship; their sanctuary. You see, the founding members had a plan.

The Plan

Through pure chance, the founding fathers of the Robalo Club had stumbled across a unique and rare opportunity – an opening in the fabric of the space-time continuum; an opportunity to own and build on a lot deep in the Ten Thousand Islands.

Somehow, the US government in its bureaucratic way of doing things had left a small parcel of the Everglades National Park in private hands, even though the vast majority was now a national park. The government intended it to be 100% government land; what they had was 99% government land – with the remaining 1% now for sale to private buyers. To this day, I don't know how it happened or who discovered the mistake. After all, who would expect anyone to be looking for land to buy in the middle of what could arguably be called a swamp? Regardless, thanks to the intersection of events, the Robalo Club now owned a waterfront lot in the middle of the private 1%. And, as it turns out, practically right dab in the middle of the Ten Thousand Islands Park.

To get there required a one-hour boat ride South from Chokoloskee. You had to traverse multiple bays – following the markers and then slowly creep thru two mangrove-canopied creeks before you emerged out at Marker #63; and there on your right was the lot – covered in thick mangroves as was the other jillion plus acres of the Ten Thousand Islands. You were in God's country because the only inhabitants were Snook and bugs; millions and millions of mosquitoes and deer fly – oh, and don't forget the poisonous snakes and fourteen-foot alligators. Of course, there was no electricity nor running water (except for the tides). To many (actually most, if not all) people, this would not appear to be the real estate deal of the century – no Louisiana Purchase – but to the Old Florida members of the Robalo Club, it was the real estate deal of their lifetimes.

You may be wondering, "What did they pay for it?" If I ever knew, I've long forgotten. It was 1965 or so when they purchased the lot and I was only four years old but you have to believe that it could barely have cost more than a few house payments on any one of their houses. It was swamp land.

So, what do you do with a mosquito-infested, mangrove-covered lot in subtropical Florida that you can only access by a one-hour boat ride from a place at the end of the road called Chokoloskee?

Not Another Campsite

You build on it. But you don't build a private version of the park service's mangrove campsites. You do it better; much, much better. You build a Snook-fishing mecca cabin with all the luxuries of home: beds, kitchen, fridge, air conditioning, shower, toilet, patio, and sofas. You remedy all the shortcomings of the traditional means of Glades camping - which pretty much relegates it to the survivalists, the hippies and those who don't know any better.

You create an oasis in the middle of the proverbial desert where Yankee canoeists from Hoboken, New Jersey, who (bug-bitten, sun-burnt and half-naked) come upon this wilderness Hilton will do or pay practically anything just for a shot of cool air, clean water and a shower. This wilderness Hilton became known simply as the Cabin.

The Cabin

The Robalo Club's plan was to build a cabin on that mangrove-covered lot on a bay known simply as Lostman's Five – meaning it was the fifth bay North of the Lostman's River (the name provides a clue to the area and the mystery and romance surrounding this special place). But not just any cabin; the cabin had to be a stilt cabin – meaning it would be built ten feet above the land (ten feet above sea level to protect it in the event of extra high tides and hurricane surges), on tall piers which must be pounded deep into the bedrock of the Earth for steadfastness.

There was nothing around but water and mangrove islands (like ten thousand of them) surrounding their lot. So, how in the world do you transport materials and conduct construction at least a one-hour boat ride from civilization? It's like ancient Egyptians building stone pyramids in the middle of the desert. Well, just as the Egyptians found a way, so did the redneck Rat Pack Robalo Club. Actually, it's pretty brilliant how these men from Florida Cracker stock conceived a plan and carved out a place for their cabin, just like the original Cracker settlers did in Central Florida, where they now lived.

First, you have to get the materials to a remote location, a very remote location. You can't move it by water from Chokoloskee; the two long creeks between the cabin and Chokoloskee are just barely wide enough for a fourteen- to sixteen-foot boat to navigate the bends and overhangs. You can airlift it in but that would undoubtedly cost money in excess of what even they were willing to pay; no matter how great the fishing. There remained one option: barge the materials in by the only route available – from the sea; more precisely the Gulf of Mexico.

The Gulf of Mexico borders the Ten Thousand Islands on the West. So the gents of the Robalo Club loaded a double wide manufactured home in two pieces, along with piers, dock materials and other equipment on a crane-equipped barge. Waiting for the perfect calm when the Gulf was smooth as glass – and no bad weather forecasts were on the horizon - they launched their building material parade of barges from Chokoloskee; but instead of going due South, they first headed West out into the Gulf.

From there, the barges followed the Florida coastline South to Lostman's River, South of the cabin. They then pushed the barges East and down the Lostman's River into the Ten Thousand Islands Park. From there, they motored North thru the various Lostman bays to the lot at Marker #63. I never heard how many days they needed to accomplish their own trip down the Nile to deliver pyramid stones but it had to be several days, at barge speed, making a large backwards "J" journey to the cabin lot.

Now comes the fun part: the redneck Rat Pack with hammers. Dad told me that each member had a part in the construction in God's Country but some of these boys (Dad included) were not that technically inclined; in Dad's case, more like technically inept. Fortunately, some of the members were quite capable in this regard but certainly they had some pros on the payroll. Yet, I want you to return to this image of the original redneck Rat Pack on a job site in the jungle – pounding piers, hoisting a double wide on to those piers and then building a dock. At the end of each day, they'd then return to the luxury accommodations afforded them at their Chokoloskee base camp, with time on their hands. Needless to say, Seagram's had a banner year that year.

Despite all odds of remoteness and lack of trained manpower, the cabin was completed, and it was a masterpiece. Even the ancient pharaohs would have been impressed. Nestled in the mangroves at Marker #63, you'd find a double wide manufactured home atop four sets of pilings; ten feet above the mucky earth. An L-shaped dock accommodated three fishing boats comfortably, with a screened-in fish cleaning house at the end of the dock. The cabin likewise boasted a screened front porch with a Weber barbeque for grilling the day's catch.

Inside was one large room – the size of a double wide trailer - with six bunks (twelve beds), two sofas, and a table for cards; all lit-up at night with gas-powered lamps around the great room. At the end was a working kitchen with a running water sink, gas-powered stove and gas-driven refrigerator. A battery-operated flush toilet, with bay water, covered sanitation; and a shower stall provided much-appreciated cleansing at the end of a hard day of sun-burnt, liquor-filled fishing.

The water system was unique in its own right. As the old Cracker settlers had done, the technical geniuses of the Robalo Club rigged a cistern system for collecting and storing water. Rainfall was collected on the tin roof and gravity-fed to tanks underneath the cabin where it was stored. Whenever there was a need for water up above, battery-powered pumps would pipe it to the kitchen or shower, as needed. It was a technical marvel but as they say, "You really don't want to see how the sausages are made." And you really didn't want to reflect on the water system knowing that you were showering in water collected from a roof where birds had been dropping their calling cards. Actually, it was not hard to put out of your mind at the end of a long, hot day of fishing.

But to top it all off was the crème de la crème: a gasoline-powered generator which powered the window unit A/C's. For the first time since the dawn of time, the Ten Thousand Islands had air conditioning. Only sex can surpass the feeling of stepping into the bitterly cold great room of the Cabin at the end of a day of heavy fishing and drinking. The boys of the Robalo Club had arrived.

Stilt Cabin at Marker #63

The Wilderness Hilton

The Cabin was totally unique. There was no equal in the Ten Thousand Islands. Yes, others had gotten whiff of the availability of private lots and purchased them but none could match the Robalo Club's Cabin. One enterprising group had gone so far as to dredge a canal for developing lots but (thank God) had fallen short and never proceeded beyond digging the canal (you can still see the straight-line canal on aerial views today).

Other groups threw up shanties; one group even beached a fifty-foot cabin cruiser up into the mangroves and used it as their fishing lodge. But nothing could boast the elegance of the Robalo Club's wilderness Hilton. (You should know that eventually they all came down – rightly so – but that comes later.)

My First Trip

Since Bobby was to be credited for getting Dad into the Robalo Club in the first place, then it was only fitting that Bobby join Dad as he took Brian and me on our first trip to the Cabin. It was Spring 1969. I was seven. Brian was five.

We were accompanied by another man, Dewey George – a worker at Edwards Packing, the family citrus business. I remember Dewey as being a hundred years old (he was probably sixty to my seven). Dewey's role would be revealed to me a little later.

It's a four-hour drive from Lakeland to Chokoloskee and I remember we got a late start so by the time we arrived at Chokoloskee, sunset was nearing and black clouds were building. Dad and Bobby quickly launched Bobby's boat and Dewey got it loaded with our provisions for three days of fishing.

Keep in mind you have to haul everything you're going to need for three days: food, fishing equipment, and the critical components of ice chests chock-full of ice and topped-off gas cans sufficient for three days of motoring. The boat couldn't have been more than sixteen feet long so with three men, three days of provisions and two boys, there wasn't an inch to spare. It wouldn't have passed a Coast Guard safety inspection but that was our vessel as we pulled away from Chokoloskee.

Being new and only seven, I knew not what to expect. I had been speckled perch (spec') fishing with my grandfather, Papa Porter, on the many lakes of Central Florida and that was really my only frame of reference. I had no idea that this boat ride was another one-hour trip, following a four-hour drive from Lakeland. And, to top it off, everything looked the same. There were no real landmarks like you'd expect on a lake: no houses, no docks, no towers, no change in the scenery. It was always mangrove-lined bays, followed by mangrove-lined creeks and mangrove-lined rivers.

That's what makes navigation so difficult and, as the sun was setting, it was apparently giving Dad and Bobby fits because with the setting sun, you now lose depth perception which compounds the navigation problem to damn near impossible without the benefit of markers. And I could tell that the identification of those markers was giving the men fits as they navigated their way for the first time in the dark.

Their navigation equipment consisted of a flood light. They would "spot" the next marker by the marker's reflector illuminated from the beam of the spot light. That reflector would provide the bearing as they drove the boat on a full plane across a bay. As they approached the marker, they repeated the process of "spotting" the next marker and made their way to it. It was like a giant "connect the dots" game on a life-size stage. The boat trip that normally takes one hour was every bit of two hours. That was Brian's and my first introduction to the place. So far, it was kinda shaping up like Dad's first trip with the mangrove campsites.

It was the next day when the majesty of the place revealed itself to me in the daylight. And I quickly came to learn the Snook fishing process in the Ten Thousand Islands. It's simple.

Since live bait is not allowed in the park, you fish with artificial baits. Artificial baits are plastic contraptions made by men to attract fish (actually they are made to attract fishermen to buy them). For Snook, artificial baits range from silver colored "spoons" with a single hook to multi-colored mirrolures of all color, sinking and diving combinations with three treble hooks (that's nine total hooks) to increase the odds of actually hanging one of those illusive creatures.

You present your lures to the fish in two basic methods: you troll or you cast. Trolling is the most basic and passive form of fishing there is. While moving the boat at slow speed, you drag an artificial bait behind you; the movement of the boat drags the lure and simulates the swimming motion of a bait. For us, this was mostly done in the narrow creeks where we had to motor slowly. Since we had no choice but to motor slowly, you might as well troll. Brian and/or I was always put on this duty. Frankly, I found it boring but our job was to hold our rods such that we dragged the lure right by the mangrove roots but not so close that we get hung up on underwater limbs. Easier said than done as the boat is constantly making sharp turns to accommodate the winding creek.

However, the creeks are beautiful because you have a front row seat with the spectacular mangroves. You see the vastness of their root structures and the creatures and fish that live amongst their water-borne roots. And when you get a strike from a Snook in a creek, hang on! You're pretty much screwed with "Snook-on" in a creek because the Snook has every advantage. In a fifteen-foot wide creek, the Snook can simply dart left or right and easily drag your line across a barnacle-covered root and slice your line in two. At least, it was exciting when the strike happened.

The second way of presenting your artificial bait to a Snook is casting. And that's how we spent ten hours each day: casting, or "chunkin' it" as David Crum Sr. called it. Being lazy, Snook don't like to work too hard for their meal. So they hide amongst the mangrove roots, preferably with a moving tide, to allow the water current to push bait fish within their immediate vicinity. Only until the bait is practically in its mouth does a Snook expend any effort. But when they do, WOW; they attack with a viciousness. And that's the excitement of catching Snook, their ambush style of feeding leads to spectacular displays and fights between angler and fish.

Mangroves – Your View When Chunkin'

Snook are fierce fighters. It's as if they attended "Shake the Lure School," as yearlings, to learn, from the BIG Snook, the art of shaking an artificial bait - even a nine-hook mirrolure, which you would think impossible. And as they mature and experience getting hooked, they simply perfect their craft. Due to their fighting prowess, you lose many more Snook than you catch.

The defensive tools at their disposal are multiple. Their first defense upon being hooked is to turn and run for the mangroves where they can drag your line across a barnacle-covered anything. Anticipating that, you have to be ready to bend your rod in an attempt to man-handle him away from the roots while not snapping your own thin line in the process. Failing that defensive stand, they're going to employ their razor-sharp gill plates which can slice not only your line but your fingers if you ever make the mistake of hoisting a Snook by the gill plate (that's one of the first things taught a fish toddler in Florida: don't put your fingers near their gills). Their third line of defense, and most spectacular, is the above-water head shake where they dance on their tails, and this is their similarity with tarpon. (Tarpon put on the same acrobatic display but pound-for-pound, Snook are the fiercest in my book.)

If you're successful in keeping a hooked Snook out of the mangroves and getting him moving toward the boat, you can certainly expect him to resort to above-the-water acrobatics, exposing the top half of his body and affording him the opportunity to violently shake his head back-and-forth to disgorge the hook. It's this fight – plus his taste – which makes Snook the most prized fish.

Yet, even if you get him to the side of the boat and you think he's tuckered out and ready to surrender, be prepared for one last burst of fight once he sees your landing net in the water. Many a large Snook has been lost at the boat – actually at the net - due to a microsecond lapse in focus by the angler. They are spectacular and practically worshipped by many a Florida angler, me being one.

This was the process presented to me on that first trip to the Glades with Dad and Bobby. Frankly, it's work. But what drives men to commit to eight to ten hours of chunkin' in the Florida heat and mosquitoes is the possibility that the next cast might yield a dance.

The Art of Chunkin'

I should speak to the art of casting because that is part of the game as well and what further motivates a competitive male to keep *chunkin' and a chunkin'*, even without the benefit of any fish action. Snook like the cover of the mangrove roots and the shade of the overhanging limbs. And the overhang of a mangrove can be extensive – several feet. So, the Snook really like to be back up amongst the roots and undercover in a place of ambush. That creates the casting challenge: getting your lure up to the mouth of that lazy Snook.

That means you become expert at darting your lure between and thru the limbs so that it lands up near where you believe the Snook are hanging. It's indeed much like throwing darts but your dart is at the end of a six-foot rod and tethered to your wrist with twenty-pound monofilament line. Casting becomes a game where you congratulate your fishing partner on how well and deep they penetrated the protective cover of the mangroves. When you're really good, you learn to skip a spoon across the water surface, like a rock, and up under the overhanging limbs.

But these nine-hook mirrolure darts can back-fire on you. The same nine hooks which are designed to snag Snook can equally snag mangrove limbs when your aim is awry. It's called "squirrel hunting" and is the embarrassing moment when you have to confess to your fishing partner that you'll need to push the boat into the mangrove limbs to retrieve the lure – which has the added bonus of generally unleashing a new horde of dozing mosquitoes.

This is what I learned on our first trip. At seven years old, I was allowed to chunk it, but only with a single-hooked spoon. One hook versus nine substantially reduced the odds of my misaim causing us to go squirrel hunting. Probably around twelve years of age, I was allowed to advance to mirrolures, which became and remain my favorite.

The process of chunkin' requires you to advance the boat down the mangrove line, seeking out where the Snook are hiding. We would cover miles and miles of mangroves in a ten-hour day of chunkin'. So you need to keep the boat moving. Today, that's done with electric kickers (trolling motors) which silently advance the boat a few yards with a touch of your toe or hand. In fact, they've become so sophisticated that they are tied into GPS where an electric kicker can hold you on a single spot or, I suppose, have the boat dance the rumba, if you so desired. Technology has really soiled the art. When we first went to the Glades in 1969, we didn't have a trolling motor. We had Dewey George.

Dewey George

Dewey George was a hard working mechanic for Edwards Packing, the family citrus business started by my great-grandfather (A.T. Edwards Sr.), expanded by my grandfather (A.T. Edwards Jr.) and now sustained by Dad (A.T. Edwards III). I don't know the arrangement Dad made with Dewey, but for two and one-half days, this quiet German man guided us along the mangrove line by virtue of rowing. That's right, rowing. Old Timers like me remember it – the lost art of propelling a boat by human muscle. Through the Florida heat and bugs, Dewey quietly rowed our boat for countless miles in search of illusive Snook. I wish I had a picture. Maybe I'll have a portrait made from these words. It deserves to be captured to canvas. It was Old Florida.

We'd chunk it all day with nothing but the sound of Dewey's oars breaking the water in a constant rhythm, broken only by the violent punctuation of "Snook-on." Yes, there was the occasional squirrel hunting, but the peacefulness of fishing deep in no-man's land, coupled with the charismatic and witty banter of Arthur Edwards and Bobby Fore, accentuated by Seagram's, was my hook. At this young age, I fell in love with the place. It was Old Florida. Anyone I've ever introduced to it – no matter the age – has experienced the same.

In writing the book, Brian reminded me that for the entire trip Dewey George kept mispronouncing mangroves as "man-goes."

Finally, towards the end of the trip, Dad spoke up, "Dewey, it's man-groves not man-goes." "No sir," replied Dewey. "When the bait goes into the woods, this man-goes in to get it. Those are man-goes." Dad stood corrected.

Get the Gun

I've spoken of Snook but no description of the Glades is complete without discussing the gators. No, not The Gators (the Florida football team) but rather alligators, the natural inhabitants and Kings over the Ten Thousand Islands kingdom.

Despite the salt and brackish water, the Glades are full of them. And the King of the Kings chose the Cabin's dock area as his throne. You see, the Cabin was the home turf of Fang – the toughest alligator in the park. Fang first appeared at the Cabin around 1970. He was big – fourteen feet long - measured by the fact that he was as long as Dad's fourteen-foot Crosby Sled. The Robalo Club membership adopted the name, Fang, due to the fact that some of his lower teeth had in fact grown through his upper jaw. Even with his snout shut, his teeth were exposed. That's one tough alligator.

Fang lived under the dock, feeding on the fish carcasses cast overboard at the Cabin's fish cleaning table. He would welcome our boats each time a new crew of drunk fishermen arrived because it signaled fresh meat for the lazy bugger. He never once caused the Robalo Club any concern until one night when things got a little out of hand.

Dad was at the Cabin with a group of eight members and guests. There had been three days of good fishing with the fishermen all packing up the next morning to begin the ride home. The sun was setting on their final day, the charcoal was heating and the whisky was flowing. All was right in the world for the Robalo Club's members and their guests. Just before sunset – and before the table was set – two guests, in combination with Seagram's, announced that they were going skinny-dipping off the dock.

They stripped their clothes, walked their white butts to the end of the dock and prepared to jump in. Just a moment before the plunge, they remembered Fang and yelled up to Dad, seated behind the security of the screen porch, "Arthur, get the gun in case the gator comes." Dad replied, "Gun hell. I'm getting my camera. I've never seen a man killed before."

Needless to say, cooler heads prevailed and we were robbed of the opportunity to receive eyewitness testimony (and photos) of Fang's reaction to two men in his living room.

As a tragic footnote, Fang was later killed. Someone shot him for sport. That's the tragic side of Old Florida – human vermin who don't value what we have each been entrusted with; instead they squander it.

Fang's Throne – Under the Cabin's Dock, 1977
(Generator Next to Screened Fish Cleaning Table - Priceless)
Brian Edwards (on dock); Gordon Waring (in boat)

Sailors' Delights

Besides Bobby Fore, David Crum Sr. was Dad's closest friend. And although Bobby accompanied us on our first trip to the Glades, no one joined us as many times as David Crum Sr., and his son, David Jr.

There's a special bond between the Edwards and Crum families – a commonality of Florida values, heritage and ethos. The Crums are Old Florida stock like the Edwards clan. They love the Glades as much as we do.

When Dad died in 2000, two people stood up to speak about Dad, David Crum Sr. and I. When I celebrated my fortieth birthday with family, the Crums were there. When brother Brian celebrated his fiftieth birthday, he did it jointly with his good friend and fellow half-centurion, David Jr. When David Jr. married his bride Patty, Brian was his best man. The bonds here go deep.

And no two men could create a more entertaining and sharp-witted team than Arthur Edwards and David Crum, especially in the Glades. It was a special treat to see them in action. They could argue about anything and you never were sure if they were serious or not but the debates were hilarious.

One on-going conflict with regards to fishing was their disagreement over which fish were considered acceptable to keep, versus throw back. Dad routinely accused David of keeping what Dad called, "sailors' delights:" small fish which old-time sailors might eat if they were far from home, with slack sails, and food provisions running low. In other words, not your prime-time fish, the throw-backs; at least as viewed in the eyes of A.T. Edwards.

One evening at the Cabin, David – one of the hardest and most accomplished fisherman I know – returned to the dock. Dad had arrived beforehand and was on the porch getting the grill lit, Seagram's in hand - and not his first for the day. David was unloading his boat when he proceeded to throw the day's catch up on the dock. Dad saw what he perceived to be some "sailors' delights" and without warning came charging down the stairs from the porch and proceeded to kick those fish into the water. A shouting match proceeded between he and David before the others could calm them down. But David tucked the experience away.

A few months later, Dad and David were back at the Cabin, similar to before but with different guests this time. David had brought a big fella – his name escapes me – but he was a Man-Mountain. If you're familiar with Junior on the old TV show, Hee Haw: the three hundred pound Bubba in overalls, that was this gentleman.

Like the scene before, the boats had been fishing in different locations all day and had reconvened at the end of the day, back at the Cabin. Again, Dad had arrived ahead of David and was preparing the charcoal in the grill. It was Déjà vu as David proceeded to unload his boat on to the dock, including the day's catch. A number of "sailors' delights" began to again line the dock. Dad saw these and came ripping out from the screened porch, ready to kick them off into the water yet again. At the last moment, just before his foot was to make the fateful kick, he hesitated and asked, "Who caught these fish?" The three hundred pound Man-Mountain in overalls replied, "Why I did." Dad's immediate response... "Damn fine fish."

David had baited him. It was brilliant, and classic.

52M23

I've introduced chunkin' it – the all-day pastime and sport of casting an artificial lure along the mangrove line, as part of the Snook hunting ritual. As I mentioned before, in our early years, Brian and I were only allowed silver spoons – namely because they only had the one hook; hence reducing the odds we'd send the boat up into the mosquito-infested mangroves to retrieve an errant cast.

But the lure of choice was the mirrolure, which had nine hooks. Unlike the simple spoon which looked like the business end of spoon, a mirrolure looked like a small fish. Three inches long, it had eyes, with painted gill plates and even some scales sketched on the side to appear as an actual bait fish. They came in every color variety known. I once asked Dad, "Dad, does the mirrolure company conduct tests to determine the best color combinations for catching fish?" Dad taught me, "No son. They conduct tests to determine the best color combinations for catching fishermen."

Dad maintained a full tackle box of mirrolures of all color combinations. But his absolute favorite was the black and gold sinker, model number 52M23. It was the first lure he pulled out of the box to start a fishing trip. And not until it failed him for a day or so would he even consider a switch. It was the ultimate lure; it would catch Snook, redfish, trout, or tarpon. Even a mangrove snapper would hit it. But its real specialty was infuriating Snook. I swear I think some Snook hit it just because it pissed them off. Dad had caught little Snook on it that were not much larger than the lure!

Because of Dad's attraction, it became my favorite go-to lure as well. You could never have too many 52M23's in your box.

Roll the clock forward forty years and I still have and use Dad's Plano tackle box. It's held up over the decades; it's crusty and smells like fish and hard-worked mirrolures when you open it. In fact, years ago I was flying to Florida from Houston for a Glades trip with Brian and cousins Rick Crumpley and Chris Webb. I wasn't about to check in my tackle box and trust it to the baggage handlers; it's priceless – with all my favorite lures and memories. So I carried it on the plane. (Of course, this was way before 9/11. It wouldn't pass security today.)

Thanks to frequent flyer points, I had been upgraded to first class and I placed the box under the seat. Mid-flight, while my neighbors were enjoying their complimentary wine and silver-china lunch with cloth napkins, I decided to check my count of 52M23's. I opened the box. Boom, the whiff of four decades of pent-up fish smell permeated the cabin. Everyone was looking around like, "What happened?" I'm surprised the oxygen masks didn't automatically drop from the ceiling. Lesson learned: don't open your tackle box in an airplane.

Just this Summer, while writing this book, my long-time friend, Paul Templin, was visiting us at Palm Island for the weekend. Late in the day, after a few beers, I suggested we head out to the North end where my father-in-law slays the Snook. I threw a couple of rods, pre-rigged with mirrolures, into the golf cart. One was rigged with the red and white 52M11 and the other one was rigged with… you guessed it, my favorite black and gold 52M23.

At the dock, the tide was ripping out; perfect for big fat lazy Snook laying up under the cover of the pier, waiting for a bait fish to follow the current - straight into their bucket of a mouth. Paul commented, "This is Snooky-looking." And it was.

I gave Paul the rod with the red-and-white lure; I kept the 52M23. On my very first cast alongside the dock – my very FIRST, a monster Snook snatched the black and gold lure and the water boiled. And of course, he did what he's built to do, he ran under the dock – spooling the light eighteen-pound test line off my reel. Before I could turn him, he stretched the line around a barnacle-infested piling and "snap" the line was cut and he was away – with my favorite and last 52M23. The old standby had done the trick, yet again.

Now the bad news. Apparently, the mirrolures company doesn't make the old 52M23 model any longer. At least, I can't find it on-line; not on the company website, not on Amazon, not on Google. I've now been reduced to hunting for used ones on eBay. That's right. That's how desperate I am. I'm buying used 52M23 mirrolures – just to feed my addiction.

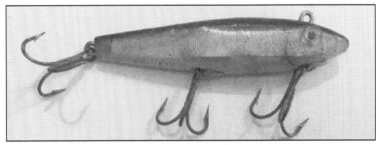

52M23 – The Snook Buster

The Canoeists from Hoboken, New Jersey

My first trip to the Glades was in 1969 when Dad gave me my first Garcia Ambassadeur model 5000 bait casting rod and reel (fifty years later I still have it, tucked away in my new Old Florida home).

By 1977, I had made eight trips to the Cabin. The annual trip was a regular Spring Break activity with Dad and his friends that Brian and I anticipated with joy each year. As a teenager, it was an incredible double treat to not only fish in the Glades but to be around grown men – especially the characters of the Robalo Club and their guests - in the wilderness. The things I observed and heard on those trips from those men could literally fill a book. They were hilarious life-learning moments that have vividly remained with me my entire life. And after eight annual trips, I assumed I had seen it all. I was wrong...

In 1977, I was fifteen; Brian was thirteen. That year's Spring Break venture was a small group of us: Dad, Brian and me, and Gordon Waring, Dad's father-in-law from his second marriage. We were at the end of a third day of all-day fishing South of the Cabin at a place called Cabbage Bay. It was a hot Florida day and our two boats were making the return run back to the Cabin.

Being the middle of the week and late in the day, with us two hours South of civilization in Chokoloskee, there wasn't another boat around; I was enjoying the drone of the motor while taking in the natural beauty as Dad navigated the turns of the barely marked route back to our Hilton. I was too young to drink but Dad had fortified his styrofoam cup with Seagram's and he was kicked back at the helm of his little fourteen-foot Crosby Sled, likewise taking in the majesty of the moment. Not knowing the route back, Gordon was trailing close behind, with Brian in his boat. They were likewise enjoying the scenic ride, anticipating the air conditioning and fresh fish for dinner.

We were within the final two-minute ride of the cabin, running the tight bends of the wide creek, when we first saw them: a small flotilla of six canoes – just ahead of us. Being a narrow space, Dad slowed the boat to no wake and slowly pulled alongside. What I saw, here in the middle of no-man's land, no doubt left my jaw open.

It was a co-ed gaggle of high school seniors slowly paddling in tandem. Given the heat, they had stripped most of their clothes: the boys had tossed their shirts away and the girls were half-naked; one had two bandanas loosely tied together as her bikini top, another only wore Hee Haw overalls with no shirt or bra. It was quite the sight for a fifteen-year-old full-blooded American male, three days in the Glades.

But that wasn't all. All of that exposed skin was bright pink from extended exposure to the savagery of the Florida sun. And, just so they truly remembered their trip, bug-bite welts covered their pink skin, making it coarse like the hide of an alligator. They were in bad shape. And yet somehow they were still paddling, like the automatic reflex of a lizards' flicking tail, even after it's dropped off. I gotta believe their naiveté over their situation is what kept them going.

Dad spoke to their adult group leader, a forty-something guy all decked out in an outfit straight from a Daktari movie, with pith helmet and all. He was the canoe tour leader and this was the tour group from Hoboken, New Jersey (I kid you not). This Yankee green-horn had gathered up kids from Jersey on their Spring Break and driven their butts to the Southern tip of Florida and launched their canoes at Flamingo, with the intention to canoe the five-day jaunt thru the Glades from Flamingo to Chokoloskee.

Their days consisted of ten hours of canoeing in the Florida sun, mostly lost, with the only bathroom break being the nearest mangrove where you could find four square feet of clear land to squat (hard to do; find the land that is). Being co-ed, I imagine that they respected bathroom privacies early in the trip but that luxury had quickly vanished after the first couple of days. After all, they were basically naked in front of each other now. It was like a scene from the TV Show, Survivor. As a matter of fact, we should have probably asked, "How many kids did you start out with?"

At night, they got to look forward to the mangrove campsites of which I've already described. Pitching their compact tents, they slept in their own sweat and enjoyed the twelve-hour symphony from swarms of hungry mosquitoes finding every two micrometer opening in the tent fabric to penetrate and extract their bloody vengeance for having dared to camp on their land. Yea, good times.

So what were the qualifications of this fella as a tour leader in the Ten Thousand Islands? Well, he had bought the book "Chart to the Wilderness Waterways" at the gift shop before embarking in their canoes. Ha. After four days canoeing and camping in the Glades, I doubt he still had the strength to count to ten thousand – let alone navigate those islands. What they thought would be a fun "get back to nature" tour had turned into the Hoboken Hellish Tour. Welcome to the Ten Thousand Islands.

As Dad assessed their situation, we gave them some water and Dad said, "If you can make it around that next bend, you'll see a stilt cabin. Come over and get out of the sun and enjoy some air conditioning." Their response was the same as a death row inmate who just learned the Governor had commuted their imminent ride on Old Sparky, up in the big house at Starke. Arms swung into motion paddling.

I gotta tell ya the look on their faces when they entered the Cabin was one of amazement. Forget the Hilton. As far as they were concerned, they had stepped into the Paris Ritz. The air conditioner was blasting away, in this oasis amidst the jungle. When Dad invited them to shower off, the girls practically stripped what remaining scant clothes they had on in the race to be the first in. During those showers, they damn near drained the tanks.

While the girls were showering, the boys were resting on our couches and tending to their all-encompassing pink sunburn and countless bug bites. Meanwhile, their fearless guide discretely pulled Dad aside, with his chart in hand, and whispered, "Can you show me where we are on this map?"

Eventually, the sun started to set and it was time for this flotilla to move on to their next port-of-call for the evening. Fortunately, they didn't have far to go. The closest mangrove campsite was just four hundred yards across the bay from the Cabin. Being that the next day was our last day, we stocked them with some provisions we could spare and saw them off from our dock.

They left slowly, with their canoes strung out between us and the campsite across the way. The last two canoes finally pulled away with the girls in each looking back over their shoulder until they were nearly half-way across the bay. As they approached their evening campsite and came within range to hear the mosquito symphony beginning to tune their instruments, I can only imagine they were trying to figure out how to mutiny and ask us for a bunk. Frankly, I was always surprised no one showed up at our doorstep that night.

I could end the story here but I should let you know that they made it out alright. The next day was our last day. As such, we always planned for a half-day fishing and then we would make our hour-long boat ride back to Chokoloskee with our few remaining gallons of gas. Their group was safely within a day's canoe trip to Chokoloskee as well.

That morning, an Easterly wind had sprung up and, in combination with an extra low tide, was blowing all of the water out of the Ten Thousand Islands and into the Gulf. By the afternoon, the unmarked channels were extremely shallow and the sand bars were frequent. It was really turning into a struggle for our boats to traverse the waterway; taking far longer than the usual hour to get back.

The canoeists had started out early for Chokoloskee that morning as we were packing up and getting in our final fishing; thus they had a jump start on us in getting back to civilization. We did eventually catch up with them, paddling away, in the Lopez River, the entrance to Chokoloskee Bay. They made it home safely and lived to tell the tale of their Hellish Everglades Tour. I'm sure they are relating it to their grandkids now. I understand only a few required professional therapy.

From Dust to Dust – End of the Cabin

The fact that the Cabin was even able to be built in the middle of a national park was a colossal bureaucratic screw-up by the federal government. They had missed some parcels in their original declaration of lands for the Ten Thousand Islands National Park. And that loop hole had created the opportunity for the Robalo Club, and others like them, to privately purchase the undeclared land. Well, the Feds weren't going to allow their mistake to go uncorrected. And the Robalo Club recognized that.

From the outset, the members of the Robalo Club knew that their time with the Cabin was limited. The government fully intended to regain those undeclared lands thru legal condemnation. Hence, from the start, the Cabin had a death sentence. It's just that no one knew how long till the execution. Just like the inmate sitting on death row in the big house in Starke, the Robalo Club pulled no legal punches in keeping their beloved Cabin from the park services' torches. They engaged Lakeland's fiercest attorneys to take on the Feds and to pull every trick known to lawyers to dismiss, dispute, and delay "this unconstitutional seizure of property" – all in a valiant effort to keep the Cabin alive for yet one more season of fishing.

The attorneys did a good job. Actually, a fantastic job in comparison to ordinary death sentence delay tactics. They kept the Cabin alive for nearly twenty years. Sometime in the mid-80's, the final court battle was lost and the Feds took the land back. The date of execution was set. And on that date, the Park Service put a torch to the Cabin.

Brian and I Return

Later in life, around 1996 when I was thirty-five or so, and after the Cabin had been burned down by the park service, Brian and I returned to the Glades. For another decade, we made annual fishing trips with friends and family to re-experience Old Florida in the Ten Thousand Islands. This time, we went as the captains instead of the crew – escorting others. Being the captain on the Wilderness Waterway forces you to really learn the place. So we did. We rediscovered the old sandbars by running aground while charting out the new ones as well.

We even caught some fish. The catch was not the same and the fish were not as big but it was mostly the place and the opportunity to escape with family and dear friends which I treasured. Any fish caught were a bonus to the trip.

Brian Edwards, Rick Crumpley, Scott Templin, Lance
Glades Trip, 2000

On one of those mid-life trips, Brian and I did get a chance to come face-to-face with a rare find. It was early morning, just before sunrise, and we were fishing in his sixteen-foot Scout boat – chunkin' the banks.

The water was like glass; we could see every movement of life. A hundred yards away, coming slowly down the mangrove-laden bank, mirroring and following the curved pattern of the shoreline was a dorsal fin; a large one, moving toward us. Brian said, "Lance, look at that shark."

Of course, our immediate response was to cast our plugs at it. It had been a slow fishing trip and we'd appreciate any type of fight at this point. In fact, sharks put up a hell of a fight and are fun to catch.

The only sound was the whirring of our Ambassadeur reels as we extended the trajectory of our casts to drop our lures right in front of the fish. No joy. Nothing. He just kept coming down the bank and towards us. Still, all we could see was the dorsal fin slowly cutting a trail thru the glass surface.

Finally, impatient and bored with this fella's refusal to play, Brian adjusted the electric kicker (trolling motor) at the bow to steer his sixteen-foot boat up close to see this thing. He pulled us right next to it. What I saw scared the hell out of me. My immediate reaction was, "Brian, get us away from this thing…"

It was as long as Brian's boat – which put it at sixteen feet. And, I swear its girth seemed as wide as the beam of his boat. It looked prehistoric. The dorsal fin was that of a shark but this was not a shark. This was the Florida sawfish. An endangered species, this creature features a five-foot snout with sharp saw teeth on each side, hence the name "sawfish." I had seen them in much smaller sizes before but never anything of this magnitude. My first thought was that this one-ton monster could take the boat out if he wanted to.

Brian ignored my preference to get the hell out of Dodge. And instead, he guided the boat right over the fish and trailed its movements as it slowly continued its path down the mangroves. Apparently, he was simply looking for his breakfast and he couldn't be bothered by us. Eventually, he dipped below the surface and out of sight.

Once I got my heartrate back in check, I thought back on an experience in this exact same fishing spot one year earlier. On that occasion, I had been fishing with cousin Rick Crumpley in his boat, chunkin' for Snook, when something large snatched my lure – and literally pulled me out of my seat and on to the stern deck. With the rod still in my hands, I gathered myself up and – with adrenaline pumping - I yanked on the rod to set the hook, expecting to commence the fight.

Instead of getting the expected concession on the other end of my line, the rod snapped in two! The object on the other end didn't budge. Neither Rick nor I had ever broken a rod on a fish before and we couldn't guess what it might have been. Now I know. I had hooked this whale a year ago and I might as well have been trying to set the hook on a tractor-trailer. I doubt he realized he was even hooked. The anticipation of these experiences, and the retelling of them over drinks, is what keeps grown men coming back.

On these post-Cabin trips, we'd stay in Chokoloskee; it was fine but not the same as being able to walk out on the dock in the middle of the night and see a billion stars – unpolluted by any lights. Or enjoying the late afternoon short ride back to the Cabin amongst the mangrove isles, knowing that we would be cooking fish on the grill on the screened porch. It was literally our Hilton in the Florida wilderness.

With our base camp in Chokoloskee, most of our fishing excursions stayed North of the old Cabin and closer to Chokoloskee. We would occasionally make the trek one hour South, back to the site to recall and recount the fun times we had in that magical place. Whenever we'd pass by the Cabin site, it was like driving past a memorial, with silent reverence. There's no evidence of its existence remaining other than our memories. The mangroves have reclaimed the spot - *As It Should Be*. The mangrove campsite across the bay is still there, with mosquitoes in full tune.

Hence, with our new base in Chokoloskee, we became quite familiar in navigating the bays and rivers between Chokoloskee and the Cabin. A favorite was the Chatham River, which is a main thoroughfare for water channeling back and forth between the Gulf of Mexico and the Ten Thousand Islands. With such a large volume of water moving in and out with the tides, we'd fish the mouth of the Chatham – a "Snooky-looking" place, with large water movements, conducive to a lazy Snook looking for a meal.

Lance and Paul Templin Fishing On The Chatham River, 2001

Death on the Chatham

I came to know the Chatham River and revisit its history in person; the history Dad had taught me so many years prior. At a bend in the river, called Chatham Bend, there's a mangrove campsite there today that originally was the farming settlement of Edgar Watson, established at the turn of the twentieth century. Just as the Robalo Club had done, Mr. Watson had carved a homestead out of the mangroves and built a two-story white frame home. But besides the home site, he had further cleared out the bend for farming. Can you imagine living and farming amongst the mosquitoes?

Mr. Watson was a tough dude. In fact, he was a bad dude. Reports are that he was an outlaw who was attracted to the remoteness of the Glades and Chatham River to escape the law. At the turn of the century, Chokoloskee had no law officer; it was a remote outpost serving those few Florida Crackers scratching a living out of the area.

Mr. Watson hired laborers to work his farm and let them live on his land at the bend. Yet, a pattern developed where the laborers would disappear without a trace and Mr. Watson would be back in Chokoloskee looking for a replacement. Suspicions began to circulate amongst the settlers in Chokoloskee that when the laborers asked Mr. Watson to be paid, he took offense and killed them. It was suspicions only; there was no proof other than missing laborers and Mr. Watson's constant need for replenishing his work force. The bodies are reportedly buried out on the bend to this day.

Just try to imagine the remoteness of Chokoloskee at the turn of the twentieth century. It was a wild island, covered in native mangroves and mosquitoes. The causeway that connects it to Everglades City on the Florida mainland did not exist. These island residents were tough folk; Florida pioneers. One of these settlers was Ted Smallwood, who operated the only trading post in that remote location.

Located on the South End of the island, Smallwood's Store boasted a dock and stilt building that contained the basics needed for human existence. As such, Smallwood's was a natural gathering place for those early island settlers. In fact, Smallwood's Store remains to this day. It's recognized as a National Historic Landmark and operated as a museum by the family – maintained in its original condition with stores of the period. You can step back into Old Florida for five dollars at Smallwood's.

Smallwood's was where Mr. Watson would dock when he made his weekly trek from Chatham Bend to Chokoloskee, to get drunk and do some trading. Given the suspicions of murder on the Chatham, everyone feared Mr. Watson. There was a tenseness when he was on the island. No one knew what he was really capable of. And again, there was no real law on the frontier of South Florida. Everyone kept to themselves, busy working in order to survive. This was the setting when a woman's body was found floating in the Chatham River.

The body was discovered by a local fisherman when Mr. Watson was at his homestead, away from Chokoloskee. It was a black woman, identified as a favorite cook among the island residents. She was endeared amongst that small remote population where everyone knew everyone. The islanders knew she had been recruited by Mr. Watson, and despite their warnings to her, she had accepted the position as his cook out on Chatham Bend.

When the news hit Chokoloskee that a favorite local had been murdered and found floating in the Chatham, everyone thought the same, "Mr. Watson murdered her. And now, he's not even bothering to bury the bodies." There was universal outrage but with no law, no action was taken. At least, no planned action was taken.

That weekend, Mr. Watson made his weekly trek to Chokoloskee and was spotted coming across the bay, steering his craft toward the dock at Smallwood's. The normal cadre of men and women were collected at the gathering place. But when word got out that Mr. Watson was coming in, others filtered to the dock to greet him, men and women. The men were each armed with a shotgun or hand gun.

There was no plan, no discussion of what they'd do. It was simply the Old Florida sense of justice coursing thru the veins of these pioneers. As birds flock together naturally from instinct, so did the men of Chokoloskee gather to confront Mr. Watson collectively at Smallwood's dock.

Mr. Watson was drunk when he tied up his boat and stepped on to the dock. He was toting his usual six-piece in his belt, a staple amongst all at the time. A voice from the crowd accused Mr. Watson, "You killed the cook!" To which Mr. Watson bowed up in his usual insolent manner to shout back, extra bold in his drunkenness, "Mind your own damn business. Get out of my way!" Watson pulled his pistol and the sound and smoke of a dozen firearms shattered the peace of the evening. Mr. Watson, the murderer, was dead; felled by Old Florida justice.

Smallwood's Store and Dock Today
Site of Mr. Watson's Demise

Dad had told me the story when I was seven or so. In fact, books have been written about it. I don't know how well my recounting of the story reconciles with the facts but I like to think that my version is *As It Should Be*.

Knowing the story, we would regularly dock at Chatham Bend - the former homestead - once each trip, and walk the exact place where Mr. Watson farmed and murdered. Of course, we would be the only people there. The old cast iron boiling pot was still there from his sugar cane curing, as well as the old water cistern. You could walk a limited portion of the homestead, reflecting on what it must have been like living in this remote, eerie place. And envision the frontier justice that occurred on Smallwood's dock.

Dad's Final Trip

During that decade of the late nineties leading into the turn of our century, Brian and I made our annual trips. Always with us were cousins from Mom's side of the family, Chris Webb and Rick Crumpley. They quickly came to love the place just as we did. David Crum Jr, who used to join us with our fathers as kids, restarted the tours as well. I invited old friend Paul Templin to experience it, and his cousin, Scott Templin. Dean Evans came in his boat on one trip. On Paul's trip, we actually hired a guide for the first time, Cecil.

Native to Central Florida, Cecil didn't show us much new with regards to fishing in the Glades but he entertained us with his singing on his large pontoon boat, fishing along the now familiar Chatham River. Scott was the first person I saw attempt fly fishing there, only to discover the winds were too much. At least, that was Scott's excuse as he took his first crack at it (I was no help at all; I just knew how to chunk it).

The only person missing in all those trips of the late nineties was Dad. And, unfortunately, circumstances never allowed for us to coordinate another trip to the Glades with Dad - until his final trip in 2001.

In June 2000, Dad was sixty years old and diagnosed with liver cancer. The doctor gave him six months. In that time remaining, I made frequent trips to Lakeland to see him. We'd watch college football together and old friends would come by and recount the good times; it brought back lots of fond memories. Thanks to Dad's brother David and wife, Bonnie, there was even a Saturday trip to The Swamp in Gainesville with Dad and my daughter, Stephanie. It was Stephanie's first Gator game and Dad's last. We sat in the same seats in which Kim and I sit today. I think of that final game with Dad each time we find our seats.

I was in Houston at the office on December 12, 2000, when Dad called and said, "I've just come from the doctor. They give me three days. Come home." I dropped everything, told my employer I had to leave and instructed my secretary to book me the next flight to Tampa as I rushed to the airport.

By early evening, I was in Dad's apartment in Lakeland, with Brian, where Dad gave us his final wishes. "I want to die here at home. I don't want to die in a hospital and I want you to make sure that happens. As far as my funeral, I want to be cremated. And I want you boys to scatter my ashes at our lake near the Cabin."

Dad's three-day prognosis extended into two weeks. Old friends came to say their goodbyes and old grievances were closed. Dad and Grandpa had not been getting along for many years and despite his own health challenges, Grandpa came to say goodbye to his oldest son.

Dad died Christmas morning in his own bed. Brian was there as well as Nana. I'm confident he held out till Christmas because he didn't want to disturb anyone's Christmas plans. In fact, I was with him Christmas Eve when I whispered to him at midnight, "Dad, it's Christmas. It's ok. You can go home now."

David Crum Sr. and I both spoke of Dad at his funeral. David spoke of Corinthians' love and the love he had for his special friend of so many decades. I recounted my favorite stories of Dad but the most impactful part of the service was Dad speaking to us from his poem of the Glades, which he had written so many years before and I read for him...

A Tale for Dicki
(As Told Summer 1980)

There is a small lake at the apex of a winding river located in the central part of the Florida Everglades. I go there to end a day's fishing. A day spent among bayou-type, desolate, mangrove bush surrounded waters, whose immense area is a maze of interlocking creeks, bays and dead-end waterways. Few men venture into this brackish water wonderland for fear of getting lost.

A great silence settles over these glades as night falls. My companion(s) are loved ones; family and friends of the rarest kind. Since early morning we have been bait-casting artificial lures in search of the incredible game fish known as Snook. It has been hot -- between the sun's rays and the water's glare, we are sunburned outside and dry inside. Our eyes are red from the squinting into the glare attempting to cast lures at tiny fishy-looking holes in and under the overhanging tree limbs. Some of the most vicious biting insects in the world have been buzzing about us constantly, having some success despite steady doses of smelly bug repellent. We are beautifully tired and splendidly sore.

It is likely no other human being is within 30 miles. There is certainly no phone, road, or electricity.

Often, we have caught fish. More often, we have not.

Anyway, I anchor the boat in my usual spot at approximately one hour before sunset, mix a large drink of whisky and soda in a styrofoam cup, lean back in my chair, take a deep breath, and behold what, for that moment, is my kingdom. Black, motionless water, flights of sea birds making for home, wild orchids bursting forth among the tangled growth. Along the jungle's edge, a patient gator's eyes and snout. Elegant porpoises roll through.

No matter the companion, little or nothing is said as we leisurely fish out the small underwater rock pile which sometimes holds fish. The sun turns from strobe light brilliant to red orange as it falls below the tree line. It's time to return to the stilt cabin ten minutes away; a haven more comforting than the world's finest hotels. I fortify the cup, weigh anchor, and cruise for home at a speed which barely planes the boat, keeping the powerful outboard at a low drone. Leaning back, I prop up my feet, behold my situation, and know that, indeed, my God is not dead.

-- Arthur Edwards

Brian and I upheld Dad's last wish. During our trip the following Spring, with cousins Rick and Chris, Dad made his final trip to his beloved Florida Everglades when we returned him to that "small lake at the apex of a winding river." There, at the end of a day spent fishing, we released his ashes.

My Stilt Cabin in the Wilderness

Recalling these stories of nearly fifty years ago has allowed me to reflect on the influences of Old Florida on my life. The Cabin and the Glades are a big part of it. Those experiences were Old Florida; a thrilling combination of the land, the people, and the times; real characters amidst the backdrop of God's country, totally and uniquely Florida. That annual Spring Break trip was something I looked forward to each year. In fact, during the Spring Break of my senior year in high school, I passed up the opportunity to go on a Caribbean cruise with my graduating class because I wasn't willing to miss a trip to the Cabin. It meant that much; not just to me but also to Brian and Dad and his closest friends, who returned with us regularly.

Interestingly, I look at my new Old Florida home today and I finally understand why I was drawn back. I've returned to those past times. I live in a new stilt cabin amongst the mangroves of Old Florida. Palm Island is that place.

Our house is built on piers fifteen feet above the ground – for the same reasons as the Cabin (hurricanes). I'm surrounded by mangroves, largely in isolation and privacy; an isolation afforded us by living on an island where the only access is by boat – just like the Cabin. And just like the old Cabin, this "new Cabin" is where family and rare friends can gather to still enjoy the rapidly vanishing beauty of Old Florida, and each other. We can be ourselves over bourbon, catching a Snook, and recounting Old Florida tales while yet creating new ones, many of which form the basis for this book.

My new Cabin even comes with mosquitoes, albeit a much tamer variety and in far lesser populations than their cousins who devoured us in the Ten Thousand Islands. In fact, my friend, Ron

LeGrand, has repeatedly commented that the wedding of Kim and I on the beach at our island was the only wedding he'd ever attended where the guests were handed bug repellant as they found their chairs on the beach. True story.

We traverse the waterways in our boat, surrounded by mangroves. We watch the porpoises, the manatees, the ospreys – just as we did in the Ten Thousand Islands. And when I get the urge after a few cocktails, I can golf cart my way to a favorite fishing spot where I can do some chunkin'; plugging away for Snook with Dad's favorite 52M23 black and gold mirrolure. No doubt the luxuries are important for Kim but, to me, it's just my stilt Cabin in paradise. And as Dad would have said, that's *"As It Should Be."*

My Stilt Cabin Today – Palm Island

The Back Story

For additional background information, audio and video interviews and/or the unpublished photos for this chapter, visit:

BONUS: The Back Story – Stilt Cabin at Marker #63
http://www.AISBbook.com/Ch01

As It Should Be

Chapter 2

Citrus, Cattle and Cash

The early Florida settlers had to make do with what they had. And in the early nineteenth century in Central Florida, they made do with what the Spanish explorers left behind: wild citrus and wild cattle. These early Crackers established the Old Florida spirit, the Cracker spirit of self-reliance, respect for the land, and respect for other men. This spirit is embodied in the Florida classics, *A Land Remembered* and *The Yearling* – later a movie starring a young Gregory Peck.

Besides establishing as their legacy the spirit of Old Florida, these early settlers, in many cases, left wealthy descendants. There are probably more "rich rednecks" (as Dad called them) in Central Florida than anywhere else in the country. My family, on both sides, was active in this citrus and cattle economy for three generations. I was the first to get out. Actually, I was forced out but that's a later story.

Central Florida is the portion of Florida known today as the Tampa – Lakeland – Orlando greater metropolitan area; or the "I-4 Corridor" to those who track voting patterns. The heart of Central Florida is Polk County, the fourth largest county in the state and home to Lakeland. Polk County is the historic Citrus

Capitol of the World, home to cattlemen and the first millionaire Cracker (Jacob Summerlin – King of the Crackers, way back in 1865!). And for seven generations, it has been home to both sides of my family: the Edwards and the Porters.

Florida Crackers settled all across Central Florida and they took advantage of the soil and heat to scratch out a living with the wild cattle left behind by the Spaniards as well as the wild citrus, likewise introduced by the early explorers. Names like Ponce de Leon and Hernando DeSoto were regular fare for me in elementary school as we learned of the search for the Fountain of Youth by Ponce de Leon and DeSoto's expeditions to claim the lands. Three hundred years later, their excursions paved the way for later Central Florida settlers.

The term "Cracker" was assigned to the Florida cowboys because of their ability to "crack" their whips with loud and deadly accuracy. Although considered derogatory by some, it is a term of endearment and pride for Old Floridians. I am from that same Cracker stock.

"A Cracker Cowboy" by Frederic Remington, 1895

On the Edwards side, my great-grandmother (maiden name Jessie Tillis, known to me as Granny) was from Alachua County. She was born in 1898 around Gainesville (Go Gators!). The Tillis family goes back far in my Florida blood line. In fact, we are distant kin to Mel Tillis, the famous stuttering and late country crooner.

Somewhere around 1915, Jessie met a dashing young man, recently migrated with his family from Tennessee, named Arthur Turner Edwards (later to become A.T. Edwards Sr.). I knew him as Papa (Edwards). Papa was the patriarch of the Edwards clan in Florida. In later years, when I was a teenager and would go to the office of Edwards Packing to visit my grandfather (Arthur Tillis Edwards, known formally as A.T. Edwards Jr; simply as Tillis), he would always take a moment to point out to me the large portrait of Papa in the foyer and remind me of our heritage, saying, "That's the man we thank for all of this." Although Tillis (Grandpa to me) was the real driving force behind the growth of the Edwards' citrus businesses, Papa was the man who got us started.

Papa (A.T. Edwards Sr.) With Blossoming Orange Tree

And it all started with orange crates. As a young man, recently migrated to Central Florida, Papa's first exposure to citrus was as a laborer. For decades in the early twentieth century, fresh Florida citrus was transported North in orange crates – wooden crates nailed together. Papa's entry into what would become his own citrus empire was building orange crates.

That humble start ultimately yielded citrus grove holdings, a packing house, a harvesting company and a caretaking business – a vertically integrated citrus operation run by the Edwards family, and respected across the state. So much so, that in 1967, Grandpa (Tillis) was appointed by Governor Claude Kirk to the Florida Citrus Commission, a body charged with the stewardship of the industry. My grandmother (Nana) would confide to me that this appointment was Grandpa's proudest moment because of his humble beginnings in Central Florida and lack of a college degree. His appointment document hangs in my study today.

It all began with the Cracker spirit and a man who nailed together orange crates. I'm sure these same stories can be told by other old-time citrus families in the state. It is the common story of Old Floridians.

Florida Fresh Citrus Crate and Label

Tillis Edwards in Citrus

Papa was in the fourth quarter of his life as I was growing up so I didn't have any direct exposure to his business life. It was all relayed to me by Grandpa and Dad. Whereas Papa was Dad's idol growing up, Grandpa was mine. Grandpa was my first model of the self-made man: confident, successful, quiet. His actions did most of the speaking for him. And when he spoke, I paid attention.

Whereas Papa started at the bottom of the citrus totem pole as an orange crate assembler, Grandpa was able to stand on Papa's shoulders to get his start. Papa wasted no time in entering seventeen-year-old Tillis into the citrus business, at the hardest possible time; the Depression-era 1930's. Things were tight and the family needed a plan to squeeze out more profits.

Papa gave Grandpa a beat-up old pickup truck with instructions to go door-to-door and buy the fruit in people's back yards. You see, in Central Florida, practically every house had a couple of orange or grapefruit trees in its backyard. And no single family could eat all of the fruit which meant most of it would simply drop and rot, creating a mess.

Grandpa solved the problem by offering to buy the fruit for nothing, in exchange for picking it, while still on the tree. It was brilliant. Besides teaching young Tillis the art of business at an early age, it provided an extra cushion of margin when even a penny was welcome. Unbeknownst to Tillis, that simple money-making side-gig is what cemented him to citrus and entrepreneurship for life.

When I was fifteen, Grandpa handed me his dog-eared paper back copy of Ayn Rand's *Atlas Shrugged* with a two-word instruction, "Read it." "Yes sir" was my auto-reply. That book, about self-made men and polled as the most popularly read book, after the Bible, had a large influence on my life. I later relayed Grandpa's same simple instructions to Stephanie as a teenager and she consumed the book as well, continuing the legacy.

Grandpa was a man's man. He was not giant in stature but he was giant in his accomplishments, at least in my eyes. At the top of the list, he was a successful entrepreneur and he planted the entrepreneurial seed in me. I was just slow on the uptake. It took to age forty before it sprouted in me; largely because I was encouraged by him to go the route he wished he had completed: a college degree leading to a vocation.

In fact, at age fifteen, Nana asked me, "Lance, what do you want to do when you grow up?" Having grown up observing three generations of Edwards in the family citrus business (Papa, Grandpa, Dad), I assumed that I was to lead the way as the oldest of the fourth generation and I replied, "Well, Nana, I guess I'll go into the family citrus business." She immediately rebuked that notion, "Nope! You can do anything you want but go into citrus. There will be no more Edwards in citrus!"

And that was that. I was out, as well as all of my cousins. Nana, in her wisdom, could see the bleak future of citrus and she was right. Today, with freezes, disease, development, international competition, and consolidation, there is no future for the individual grower. Disease alone, known as "greening" with no cure, will likely bring the death knell.

Life in Citrus

A few years ago, after Dad and Grandpa had both passed, I asked my Uncle David – the last Edwards still active in citrus - what did the economics look like for an orange grove. As an entrepreneur by this time, I was curious; I was actually entertaining thoughts of buying a small orange grove just for the sake of my Old Florida roots. David gave me a quick education on grove economics and finance. At the conclusion, I looked at him kind of bewildered and asked, "Why would anyone want to get into the citrus business?"

Besides the tough math for anyone looking to enter the industry, it's a low return business with high risk – not an attractive pairing. Setting aside the real risk of disease, there's the pervasive freezes which can take out not just your crop but the entire grove. And given that it takes five years for a new tree to produce a single orange, that's a long time to go with ZERO income.

As a youngster, I can remember the family watching temperatures drop on Christmas Eve gatherings; the adults wondering if this year was going to be an economic bust and if they could afford the gifts already under the tree.

In the old days, growers would burn old tires in the groves as a heat source against the pending freeze. It was common to see black tire cores piled high in groves as the inventory for the next freeze. The EPA ultimately took exception to burning tires and growers switched to more expensive smudge pots; oil-burning kettles which were likewise placed strategically around a grove to fend off sub-freezing temperatures.

Just imagine the manpower that has to be unleased on (maybe) forty-eight hours' notice that a freeze is imminent. As with the tires, the smudge pots met the same fate as the EPA flexed its muscle. I remember Grandpa fighting that one, "We are not polluting the air. We are trying to save the trees which produce breathable air."

Smudge Pots Firing an Orange Grove

After a freeze hit, I'd ride with Dad thru the frozen groves and he'd pull fruit off the tree and cut it with his thin-bladed citrus knife to evaluate the extent of the damage. When water freezes, it expands, unlike most liquids which contract as the temperature drops. So, in a freeze, the water in oranges and grapefruit expands to burst the cells, yielding a mushy interior. Soon the fruit will start to drop and rot.

It was in this critical week after a freeze that the family would scramble to harvest as much fruit as possible before it dropped and rotted. The fruit could not be sold as fresh produce but it could be sold as juice for concentrate. I suspect many growers push plenty of dropped (and rotting) fruit after a freeze. After all, that crop probably stands between them and bankruptcy. That's the life of a citrus grower, and the life the Edwards family chose to embrace for three generations.

When you take it all into account, it's easy to understand why so many growers opt to sell their groves to a developer, to have the acres and acres of orange trees replaced by tract homes or the ubiquitous mobile home trailers (which, as Jimmy Buffett rightfully sings, "Looked a lot better as tin cans"). The increased frequency of freezes drove the industry farther South into the state until ultimately Polk County lost its distinction as the Citrus Capitol of the World – a recognition which Grandpa and the rest of the Edwards family presided over for three generations.

Polk County Citrus Center Marker (Erected 1930)

The Boom

During its heyday, citrus was everywhere in Florida. Citrus stands were found on every highway in and out of state. Owned and operated by Mom and Pop Crackers, this was their self-made empire, their legacy bounty from the original trees left behind by the Spanish and organized into an industry by early settlers and men like Grandpa. At the citrus stand, you could load your car with citrus of every variety and top it off with souvenirs and trinkets (soon to be lost) memorializing your trip to sunny Florida.

Orange trees were always within view. They were not only in the ever-present groves but in our school yards and homes. We had two trees in our back yard on Polk Avenue: an orange tree and a grapefruit tree. We'd eat a few pieces of fruit but mostly it was a chore for Brian and me to pick up the dropped and rotted oranges because we simply couldn't eat that many. When we were really enterprising, we'd pick the green oranges and cover the sphere entirely in dripped wax. It makes a hard ball and perfect for games of "bean your neighbor" with the other boys in the neighborhood. Keep in mind, we didn't have helmets. We just found it great sport to leave red welts on each other in our version of "War." (We didn't have iPhones or video games. We had nature to occupy our time.)

When you traveled along the Florida Ridge on Highway 27, you were overtaken by the breath-taking view of miles and miles of orange groves across the hills along the ridge. In Clermont, the Citrus Tower was built (and still stands) so that for fifty cents, you could ascend the height and take in the view of miles and miles of neatly lined orange trees across the white canvas of sand. I have a poster hanging at home. It was a sight.

Citrus Tower, circa 1960's

We had the Orange Bowl, the Citrus Bowl, the Tangerine Bowl. We had parades and citrus queens. In Winter Haven, there was a round building shaped like the hemisphere of an orange-half and painted orange across its entirety. For my high school prom, Dad arranged for me to take my date to the Citrus Club in Orlando (a rare treat for a seventeen-year-old but an unnecessary one-hour drive from the festivities).

When Disney World opened in the early seventies, it boasted a Florida Citrus stand with original Florida orange juice. The exhibit was located at the entrance to Adventureland, on the side toward the Swiss Family Robinson Tree House. Today, it's been replaced by some singing robotic birds or other nonsense. Grandpa was instrumental in getting that citrus stand inside Disney World and for Christmas that year, he gave me a Mickey Mouse watch; a gift from Roy Disney to him. The chairman of the Florida Citrus Commission said it was "the most significant event in citrus history."

Orange Bird at Disney World
Created by Disney for the Florida Citrus Commission

We drank orange juice at every school-served lunch in elementary school. Packaged in small triangular shaped cartons with a punch hole for the straw, I used to grimace at the moment of drinking that concentrate. I thought it was terribly bitter. Nevertheless, the school district served it; thanks to the marketing prowess of the citrus industry. It was so bad, as a youngster I once asked Dad, "Dad, do I have to like orange juice to go into the orange business?" "No son," was his reply with a smile.

Grandpa was riding the boom. He used the cash flow from the booming citrus business to purchase groves, beach homes, airplanes, boats, and ranches. He parleyed his knowledge of the industry into plays in the citrus futures market, a hedge against crop risk, and a contest of his mind against other men to bet on the year's citrus crop estimate. For all the time I knew him, I never once saw him in a grove. Dad was the one driving the groves in his "grove car" – a new Oldsmobile perpetually scratched from the tree limbs, with orange leaves and twigs in the back floorboard where he'd gathered oranges from various trees to test for sugar content and ripeness at the office; a sugar measure known as brix. (I later learned the same acid titration process in my freshman chemistry class at Duke.) A large whip radio antenna attached to his bumper, and his dash-mounted radio was his communication vehicle back to the truck dispatcher at the office. Of course, there were no cell phones. When the family would go to the Lakeland Drive-in Theatre in Dad's grove car, I remember the sound of the eight-foot antenna rubbing along the bottom of the covered roof at the drive-in ticket entrance.

While Dad and Uncle Mike worked the groves and managed the picking crews and the packing house, I could always find Grandpa at his desk. It was an impressive office, representative of the man. Large animal trophies encircled the large office; reminders of his Canadian hunting trips to the Yukon where he'd bag rams, moose, dall sheep, and even a brown bear. They were all there in his office – even the bear, fully stuffed in standing position and paws raised. Today, "the bear" stands proudly in Uncle David's office, the last Edwards involved in citrus.

Grandpa's position at his desk was always the same: phone to his ear, elbow to the desk; conducting business with someone or giving futures trading instructions to his broker. I remember him once commenting at the end of a day, "Well, I just paid for the new boat today."

When I was able to drive and had wheels, I'd sometimes drive out to the office unannounced, just to be around the man. He was always busy. Yet he always welcomed me. We didn't talk much. He was too busy and he was not the easiest man for me to talk to. I just wanted to be around him, especially proud of this part of my heritage.

Grandpa (Tillis Edwards) and His Bear, circa 1975

Betting It All

It's been said that the first generation starts a business and the second generation grows it. That was the case with the Edwards family's citrus business. From his start as a citrus crate builder, my great-grandfather (Papa) boot-strapped his way to become a citrus millionaire (back when a million dollars was a million dollars). He was Edwards Groves. Dad would tell me that everyone knew that "all you needed was the handshake of Arthur Edwards Sr. in any business transaction."

Papa Edwards was the classic success story of the self-made man: work hard, be disciplined and always do the right thing. The prime period of his reign was the 1920's thru the 1940's. Prompted by my new-found learning of the Great Depression as a youngster, I once asked the patriarch, "Papa, how did you do in the depression? What was it like?" Normally a quiet and reserved man, he looked at me and recalled the boom Florida period of the 1920's leading up to the crash in three sentences, "There were a lot of boys telling me,

Arthur come get this easy money. Well, I resisted. And we were okay." I was left to fill in the blanks from there.

Easy money was an oxymoron for Papa and Granny Edwards. They worked hard for everything they had and couldn't relate to anything "easy." For example, even into her nineties, Granny tended to her vast pineapple garden at her country home. Granny and Papa were the ones who set up the old-fashioned passbook savings accounts for Brian and me and all of our cousins, as newborns. That was them: plant a seed, tend to it and let nature take its course. That was their basic philosophy. They exemplified that philosophy in their "garden" – a one-acre mini-farm they tilled into their eighties. It was a real treat to be given produce from the garden because it was the best there was.

When in season, Brian and I especially looked forward to the privilege of picking and eating Granny's sweet blackberries - but not all of them; she had a special purpose for her home-grown berries. Fifty years later, I suppose it's now safe to let on to Granny's little secret. A teetotaler, who never took a sip of liquor to my knowledge, Granny prided herself on her bootleg blackberry wine which she covertly stilled in her garden shed. The revenuers never caught on.

Granny (Jessie Tillis Edwards) and Papa (A.T. Edwards Sr.)
Notice The Handmade Fishing Poles (Tree Limbs), 1920's

Late in her life, after Papa had passed and Granny had nary a financial care in the world, she pulled Mom aside one Christmas season and said, "Now the boys shouldn't expect too much for Christmas this year, I had to replace the pump in the well." When Mom gingerly confided this to Grandpa, he laughed, "Ha, she could buy the company that makes the pumps." Granny and Papa were Depression era people. All they knew was hard work and saving.

Granny and Papa (circa 1975)

While driving with Grandpa across his ranch one cold morning, he recounted to me how the family got thru the Depression when things did get tight. Deep into the Depression, Papa had pulled Grandpa out of Florida Southern College to come help run the business (where believe it or not, my grandfather was studying to become a dentist). Revenues had dropped and the business was facing a crisis, a financial shortfall. Papa gathered his brother, Ralph, Granny's nephew Clifford, and his twenty-year-old son, Tillis, around the table to discuss the problem, "What are we going to do?"

The men looked at each other and Grandpa held his tongue in respect to the elder men's opinions. When nothing solid was offered, Grandpa spoke up with confidence, "Dad, here's what we're gonna do. First, we are going to lay off everyone except the bookkeeper. Then we're going to cash in your $50,000 life insurance policy to use as our seed capital to restart." And that's what they did; all from the mind of twenty-year-old Tillis Edwards. They bet it all.

From that "all in" bet, Tillis expanded the simple family business that began from nails and wooden orange crates to its apex of orange groves, a packing house, a harvesting company and a caretaking business; what would be called at Harvard Business School today a vertically integrated citrus operation.

Grandpa had no business training whatsoever. He just had a great heritage, immense common sense, and guts - plus the ability to learn what he needed to know. Ultimately, that twenty-year-old college drop-out, who led the expansion of the family citrus business over three decades, was trusted by the governor with the entire industry; just another Old Florida self-made man.

Reminders of a Simpler Time

The citrus industry has little resemblance to those breakthrough decades of the 'twenties thru the 'seventies. The individual grower has largely been pushed out by consolidation, freeze, disease and international competition. But from the period of the 'twenties thru the 'forties, there remains for us reminders of what it was like during the heyday of a nascent industry. You see, affixed to those same wooden orange crates, where my great-grandfather got his start, were citrus labels.

Each grower had its own unique design for its citrus brand and that brand was printed on a label pasted to the end of each crate. Just as Coca-Cola has its brand, so did hundreds of individual growers across the state. Colorful, yet simple, these citrus labels were created in the period long before desktop publishing. Often funny, they centered around themes of Indians, royalty, birds, or flowers. There were brand names such as: Blue and Gray (after the Civil War), Gasparilla (after the Tampa Bay pirate), Cracker Girl, Cracker Boy, Jack-S, Silver King (after the tarpon), and Florida

Cowboy. And, of course, the Edwards family had citrus labels for their fresh citrus brand.

Partial collections of the Edwards' labels are scattered across the family. Uncle David has an original hanging in his den. Mom found me another original years ago which hangs in my Houston office. My cousin, Julie Edwards Pivovarnik, decorated her new home with them. In researching for the book, I scored a coup when I found them all online at the University of Florida's Citrus Label collection. What a treasure trove. In fact, I even discovered one which I had never seen before. Today, all of the Edwards' labels hang at our home in Florida.

Edwards – Pritchett - Tillis Citrus Label, 1936

During the time I was writing this book, Kim was dragging me (literally) thru a little furniture shop in Sarasota one Saturday afternoon; one of those places that carries refurbished furniture, cute cookie plates and other stuff totally of zero interest to me. I was working my best at being patient and a good husband, wandering the store on my own, trying to feign interest. And then I saw it...

Way in this small back room with an overpriced and refurbished dining table, loaded with stacks of unsalable stuff; there was tossed casually at the top of a tall bookshelf, out of reach to most and almost out of sight... an old wooden citrus crate with its original citrus label intact! I couldn't believe it. This was the same exact type of citrus crate which my great-grandfather built as his entry into citrus one hundred years ago. From my recent research, I immediately recognized the label; it was the Aunty brand out of Polk County, specifically the city of Bartow – a few miles South of Lakeland.

I pulled the crate down and quickly walked to the front of the store where the manager was fastidiously checking out some ladies with their French tea cups. "I'll give you a hundred dollars for the crate," I said, and pulled out a Franklin. "Well sure," he replied, somewhat shocked. After he rang me up, he said, "I'm surprised you paid a hundred dollars for this." My reply, "I'm surprised you didn't hold out for a thousand. I would have paid it."

It Takes Two

My citrus heritage is not one-dimensional. It spans across both sides of my family. Mom's maiden name is Porter and like the Edwards, my great-grandfather Porter brought his family to Florida in the early twentieth century. Originally hailed from Missouri (pronounced Mi-zur-a to that state's natives), they likewise resided in Polk County in an even smaller town than Lakeland called Bartow.

Now here's where it gets a little confusing. Whereas my great-grandfather Edwards went by Papa, my grandfather Porter also went by Papa. So we had Papa Edwards and Papa Porter. Papa on Mom's side was Paul Milton Porter.

At age twenty-three, Paul married sixteen-year-old Gladys Howze (Porter), my grandmother who I knew as Mama. Shortly after marriage, Mama's mother died in childbirth and Mama agreed to raise her young sister, Janiece - quite a responsibility for a sixteen-year-old newlywed to take on. The year was 1927 and a depression was on the way.

Mama's family lived South of Bartow in Ft. Meade, named after the fort established during the Seminole Indian Wars, just as Fort

Myers and Fort Lauderdale derive their names. In the frontier Florida days of the mid-nineteenth century, these were the string of forts by which semi-safe passage was made across the state, connecting the inland with the Gulf and Atlantic ports – with each fort separated by a distance of 15-25 miles, considered a day's travel for horses, wagons and marching troops. Ft. Fraser was between present-day Lakeland and Bartow. As way of trivia, young Stonewall Jackson – the brilliant Confederate general – was stationed at Ft. Meade in 1851.

Paul and Gladys ultimately moved to Lakeland, and raised their family in the same house where Mom was born, on Ruby Street near Lake Hunter. They lived the rest of their lives in that single home.

Young Paul Porter and Gladys Howze, 1926
(Of Course Fishing)

Papa Porter was my fun grandfather; the one who took Brian and me fishing regularly and allowed us to discover Central Florida lakes. The one who played football and baseball with us. The one who let me operate the stick shift on his red Ford pickup when his shoulder was aching. And the one who slipped five dollars into my empty wallet when I would sleep overnight at their house.

Raised in the Cracker spirit of early twentieth-century Central Florida, the Porter family were very proficient in making their living off the land. They operated a dairy with my grandmother's family – the Howze's (J.A. Howze Farmside Dairy) in Ft. Meade. At the dairy, Papa did it all: he milked the cows, bottled the milk, and cleaned the barns.

In my research for the book, I stumbled across an ad for a 1930's milk bottle from the family dairy, which sold on eBay for $81. And, just as I did with the chance discovery of the old citrus crate, I immediately emailed the seller of the milk bottle and offered him much more. Mom has two bottles she's found over the years.

1930's Milk Bottle from
J.A. Howze Farmside Dairy; Ft. Meade, Fla

Papa was an avid hunter and fisherman. He loved catching 'specs, otherwise known as speckled perch (or crappie in Georgia). He always owned two or three boats, one which worked and one or two others in various stages of fix-up or repair. And short of the nuclear machinations of a US submarine, I don't think there's anything he couldn't fix or build. When anything broke, my retort as a youngster was, "Ask Papa. He can fix it."

Seriously, over the twelve years I knew him, he operated an auto mechanic shop and a body shop. He was a master mechanic. And a master carpenter who built the octagonally shaped steeple at the Catholic church in Lake Wales because his super didn't know how. He'd always point it out to me on our drives to Camp Mack at Lake Kissimmee.

Not bad for a man who had to drop out of school in the eighth grade to help support the family. He was a true self-made man. When he decided he wanted to open a body shop, he secured an auto body repair job where he could learn the trade. Once he felt he knew the basics, he jumped off on his own. What courage. What a spirit.

Papa Porter's Handiwork - The Octagonal Steeple

When Mom wanted to enclose our carport and convert it to a "Florida" room, Papa sketched up some plans and did it. When Mama wanted to add a room extension to their house on Ruby Street, he built it. When his boat punched a hole in the bow below the waterline on Lake Kissimmee one cold December morning, he fixed it (but that's a later story). For a stint, he was even a mechanic at Edwards Groves.

Whereas Grandpa Edwards planted the seed of entrepreneurship in my mind, Papa Porter planted the "builder" seed which later blossomed into a Master's degree in Chemical Engineering and a successful twenty-year corporate engineering career.

The entrepreneurship seed finally blossomed around age forty, and launched a successful business recognized by Inc. Magazine as one of the fastest growing private companies in the United States three years in a row. Just as Grandpa stood on the shoulders of his father, I stood on the shoulders of my two distinct grandfathers, both of Old Florida.

Papa (Paul Porter) and Hunting Dog, 1930

The Birds and the Bees

Papa Porter was his own self-made man. And he entertained us continually with his stories, his laugh, and his adventures. He could talk to anyone. And in addition to all of the above attributes, he was likewise a citrus man - a gentleman citrus grower.

Papa owned a twenty-acre grove down in Lake Placid, South of Lakeland - population 2,000. There wasn't much to Lake Placid besides the highway and orange groves. As with everything, Papa maintained his own grove. In fact, he planted every tree himself. He did the caretaking, the pruning, the fertilizing and built his own spray machine for spraying. It was just yet another of his countless skills. I would occasionally accompany him down to his grove. He'd drive the sandy rows in his red pickup; he'd inspect things, tinker with the pump in the pump house and generally just check things out. Frankly, there's normally not much to do in an orange grove, outside of picking season, other than watch it grow and perhaps run off some Yankee tourists trying to pick your fruit. It was just fun to be with him.

In the corner of his grove, in a cleared area, down by the lake, there were stands of white wooden cabinets, in four stacks about five feet tall. "What's that?" I asked Papa. Papa explained, "Those are bee hives Son. I let the man who owns them keep them there. The bees pollinate the orange blossoms so I have a good crop and the bees use the blossom nectar to make their honey, which that bee man gives me as rent."

That was my first introduction to the birds and the bees. And without really understanding it at the time, it was my first lesson on the land and the delicate symbiotic connection between everything; the plan put in place by Mother Nature and loaned to man for his stewardship - a lesson lost to too many intruders in the fifty years since. More on that later.

Cattle

Besides citrus which was left behind by the Spanish explorers, the early Florida Cracker settlers found another legacy of the Spanish: wild cattle. In 1521, Ponce de Leon tried to establish a colony on present-day Pine Island at Charlotte Harbor, South of our home. Although the Calusa Indians saw to it that the colony didn't make it, the attempt saw the first introduction of cattle to Florida, the ancestors of a hardy variety which came to be known as the Cracker Cattle breed.

Florida Cracker Cattle Breed

The Central Florida prairies provided natural grazing for the wild cattle and the warm weather was hospitable to settlers. Cattle was another foundation upon which lives were sustained and fortunes made.

Most people outside of Florida associate the state with beaches, citrus, and/or the mouse in Orlando but few realize the cattle connection. In fact, much of the land now inhabited by trinket shops around Disney was originally cattle land – as was Disney World itself. And for six generations prior to me, my family has been raising cattle (along with citrus) in this area of Central Florida.

For years, Mom has researched our genealogy from her side (Porter) up to the Howze's and Alderman's. Without elaborating on who begat whom, let me just say that those families spit out children like rabbits. My great-grandmother, Gertrude Alderman Howze, had eleven siblings. My 3X great-grandfather, Timothy Alderman, had fourteen! All necessary when you are self-made Florida pioneers living off of the land and you need all hands on deck.

Mom's research is impressive and makes for proud reading as a descendent. Here's just some highlights which may be of interest: My 4X great-grandfather, James Alderman, was the first white man South of the Alafia River in the Indian territory of Hillsborough County. A true Florida pioneer, he homesteaded the land in 1848 and established the ford at the Alafia River for all later wagons. That area is now a popular Hillsborough County Park aptly named Alderman's Ford Park.

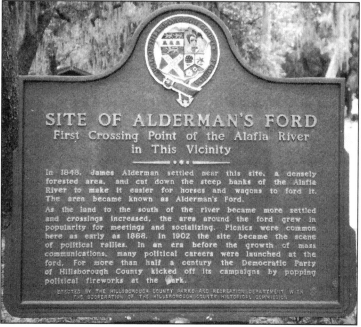

Marker at Alderman's Ford Park

Florida had been a state for just three years when James arrived in 1848. Central Florida was literally a wilderness, no different than the American West, with the constant threat of another Seminole Indian war outbreak (which occurred in 1855 with the Third Seminole War around Ft. Meade and Ft. Fraser). Six years prior, Congress passed the 1842 Armed Occupation Act which offered 160 acres of Florida land to any able-bodied man willing to move to Central Florida, under two stipulations: one, you must own a gun and know how to use it and two, you could not homestead within two miles of a fort. Bottom line: you were expected to help tame Florida on your own. And that's where James Alderman found himself in 1848.

Pioneer families homesteaded along rivers and streams just like James Alderman did along the Alafia River. These few hardy dream-seekers were willing to risk everything and take a chance in Florida. That cracker spirit and "bet it all" approach was repeated over and over by my ancestors and many just like them. They all shared the common goal to carve out a better life in the Central Florida wilderness. It wasn't until 1849, one year after James Alderman settled, that the Central Florida territory was opened up to official settlement, still under the watchful eye of the Army.

Alderman's Ford at the Alafia River. Untouched
(Location is Best Guess Per Historians)

My family's story in Central Florida begins at the birth of the state and even before the birth of Polk County. In fact, Polk County would not be formed (from Hillsborough and Brevard Counties) for thirteen more years in 1861 – one month after Florida seceded and left the union. And, my ancestor, James Alderman, was there as one of the signors of Florida's secession papers.

James' descendants would settle across Central Florida, including Mulberry and Ft. Meade, all industrious in cattle and citrus. It is from my Alderman line that I can make my claim as a seventh-generation Floridian. My 3X great-grandfather, Timothy Alderman, served with the Cow Calvary during the Civil War to supply the Confederate Army with much-needed Florida Cracker cattle.

Timothy Alderman, Confederate Cow Calvary Soldier

Timothy's son, David Alderman, was my 2X great-grandfather and get this… his wife, my 2X great-grandmother's birth name was Florida Beulah Waters. That's right, *Florida*. (Her sister was named Georgia. I kid you not.) Our Old Florida roots go deep.

Marriage License: David Alderman to Florida B. Waters, 1888

Double Diamond

I came to know the beauty of this unadvertised aspect of Florida's cattle history through Grandpa Edwards' own cattle ranch, the Double Diamond. Located near Polk City, in Polk County, I could ride with Grandpa in the comfort of the heated cab of his four wheel drive truck and experience native and untarnished Florida, just as I did in the Ten Thousand Islands with Dad. This was real Florida – just as the Spaniards found it, as did the first Crackers.

It's beautiful country; acres of flat pastures, interrupted by "pine islands," swamps and creeks. As a lone island in a sea of grass, "pine island" is the literal description of these large isolated clumps of tall pine trees, one hundred-year-old moss-covered oaks, palmetto plants and under-growth. Largely unchanged for eons, I could step back into time by a simple visit to Double Diamond.

Besides the wild cattle which could be found on the prairies, the pine islands were abundant with game: deer, bear, bobcat, wild hog, fox, armadillos, possum, raccoons, quail, and all types of snakes - venomous and otherwise; plus the Florida panther. On the brink of extinction today, the Florida panther is a kin to the mountain cougar and largely restricted to the Southern reaches of the state, where it is strictly protected. The other game has diminished in numbers as well, reduced due to the robbery of its native habitat, by development - and over-hunting.

I sought every opportunity to visit Old Florida at Double Diamond. In Boy Scouts, Grandpa allowed us the use of the ranch for our regular weekend camping trips. He operated the land as a working cattle ranch, but I suspect he owned it for the same reason he owned a beach home; it put him closer to the land which he loved as well, plus it provided him the opportunity to hunt. Among his many achievements, he was an accomplished hunter and he often hosted deer hunts on the land for his close friends where Brian and I would be invited on occasion. He'd hunt quail there as well, with his hunting buddy of many years, Jim Boone.

Skunk Ape

Besides finding sprawling acres of pine islands and prairie in Central Florida, there are swamp hammocks: water bogs with cabbage palms and tall straight cypress trees which butt up to the prairies and hold game and other wildlife.

Cabbage palms are a variety of palm tree where the trunks are covered from ground to head in broken-off palm limbs. Cabbage palms are also the source for swamp cabbage (otherwise known in finer establishments as heart of palm). Heart of palm is actually the better descriptor because swamp cabbage is the inner trunk of a cabbage palm. It was Nana's second husband, my Yankee step-grandfather Robert Safford, who introduced me to harvesting swamp cabbage. It's a lot of work. First, you shuck the dead palm stalks surrounding the trunk. Once you've exposed the bare trunk and drenched yourself in sweat, you then hatchet your way to the inner soft core where you harvest your prize.

I can't imagine the number of palm trees that are killed for the sake of that core. But I can see the early Cracker settlers surviving on the palms as their sustenance, along with the other wildlife abundant in the hammocks. Even the palmetto plants are edible, as I learned camping at Double Diamond with my Boy Scout troop.

As far as surviving on the hammock wildlife, Boy Scouts also taught me that armadillos, prehistoric-looking and quite fast, are good to eat. We chased one down once at a Double Diamond camping trip and barbecued it. Of course, that was before anyone knew they can carry leprosy. As I recall, it tasted like chicken (of course).

Where the ground gets boggy, you find the tall cypress trees, the sentries to the swamp. The cypress trees are protected and encircled by their natural uproots called "cypress knees" which are best described as roots above ground. These dulled spikes, six to eighteen-inches tall, make travel thru a swamp difficult, not that you'd want to be in there too deep due to the water moccasins and other critters. In fact, there's a special swamp critter, unique to Florida that you want to look out for – the Skunk Ape.

The Skunk Ape lives in the Green Swamp, the area West of Double Diamond and North of Lakeland. Totally isolated and protected by thousands of acres of native prairies, pine islands and swamp hammocks, the Skunk Ape has only been seen on limited occasions. Born of folklore and rare sightings, the Skunk Ape is cousin to Bigfoot, Sasquatch and the Abominable Snowman. A tall, upright-walking ape-like creature – who stinks like a skunk - he's alleged to be the thief of dogs from rural homes surrounding the Green Swamp.

I remember in the seventies reading in the local newspaper (the Lakeland Ledger) the story of the Green Swamp redneck who heard the creature in his storage shed one night and shot the ape "three times in the chest with my 30-06 rifle. He just walked away." I recall thinking that's one tough critter. Of course, no blood was found on the scene but an empty fifth of bourbon was discovered in the shed. I guess the fella misaimed - because no real Floridian doubts the creature's existence.

The legend goes back generations. Uncle Mike raised my cousins, Scott and Jay, on the tale of the Skunk Ape. Jay later wrote, directed and released a movie featuring the critter (gorilla suit and all). Titled, "Stomp! Shout! Scream!," the movie was filmed on Anna Maria Island and Egmont Key, a barrier island and key I'll introduce in Chapter Four.

Two of the film's characters are named after my grandparents. Nana even has a cameo in the movie. You can buy it on Amazon – while supplies last.

The Legend of the
Skunk Ape Lives On

The Back Story

For additional background information, audio and video interviews and/or the unpublished photos for this chapter, visit:

BONUS: The Back Story – Citrus, Cattle and Cash
http://www.AISBbook.com/Ch02

Chapter 3

Bone Valley Gold

Besides citrus and cattle, there was gold to be found beneath the ground of Central Florida by the pioneers – at least, a kind of gold: phosphate.   Phosphate is the naturally occurring derivative of phosphorous (found in our bones) and is used in the production of fertilizer. Twenty-five percent of the world's phosphate is mined in the Bone Valley region of Central Florida.

Ten million years ago, Florida was covered in sea water. Even before the Skunk Ape, other unusual Florida critters roamed the sea above where we live now. And over millions of years, the sediment from the bones of those dead creatures accumulated on the sea bottom to form today's mineral deposits. Those unusual critters were the founders of Florida's phosphate industry. That dying fish from one million years ago would carry through to connect everything that we see today. Its death would touch the lives of my family and those of my wife, Kim.   Everything is connected.

My Yankee step-grandfather, Robert Safford (Uncle Bob to me), the same man who introduced me to swamp cabbage, was a respected engineer to the phosphate industry for decades. Trained at Cornell and Yale with a Master's degree in Chemical Engineering, Uncle Bob was a brilliant engineer who had a huge influence on my life. Setting yet another entrepreneurial model for me to follow, Uncle Bob worked his way up the corporate ranks of the phosphate industry to become Chief Engineer to the leading companies. He later traded that ladder for the freedom of self-employment when he ultimately went out on his own as a leading consultant to the industry.

Uncle Bob (Robert Safford), 1970's

When Nana proclaimed to me at age fifteen, "No more Edwards will go into the citrus industry," that set me on a search for something else. Desiring to return home to Florida following what I assumed would be a four year college stint out-of-state, I told everyone I wanted to be a chemical engineer to the phosphate industry. Initially influenced by Uncle Bob, I selected chemical engineering as my field of study for a number of other reasons: it satisfied my analytical nature; it was the most difficult major; and most importantly, it paid the highest starting salary of all undergraduate studies.

In 1984, I graduated with my Bachelor's degree in Chemical Engineering from the University of Houston. I had been sponsored by Jacobs Engineering in Lakeland - a major engineering supplier to the phosphate industry. Dad had gotten me summer gigs at Jacobs as a draftsman while I was home from college. Each Summer, the drafting rooms were abuzz with rows and rows of men at their drafting tables, hand-drawing blue prints for new and/or expanded phosphate plants. Of course, there was no such thing as computer aided drafting; you had a T-square and your lead pencils. The phosphate money was flowing. I think I made seven dollars per hour in 1981 - great summer money for a college student; it kept me flush in beer and beach trips with my good buddy, Paul.

The agreement with Jacobs was that they would pay my tuition to the University of Houston – a top ten chemical engineering program – and get me a part-time draftsman job in their Houston office. In exchange, I would give them two years' employment in Lakeland upon graduation. Given that my goal was a chemical engineering job in the Florida phosphate industry, I signed up; it was a no-brainer.

In August 1981, Mom provisioned me with a U-Haul full of clothes and apartment furnishings, plus six hundred dollars cash (which she couldn't afford). I drug that U-Haul to Houston behind my 1968 Mercury Cougar; watching the engine temperature gauge more than I watched the speedometer. I was nineteen.

That trip is a milestone date for me because it came to mark the date upon which, unbeknownst to me, I was on my own financially. I suppose if I knew beforehand what really awaited me in Houston, I would have been far more nervous. Nevertheless, I made it. And I've paid my own way ever since that fateful drive to Houston. I like to think that the Florida Cracker spirit is flowing in my veins as well.

I never worked harder than I did during those three years at the University of Houston (UH). UH was a top ten program and proud of it. Their chemical engineering curriculum was designed to weed out seventy-five percent (75%) of the entering class! I carried a full course load, and on top of that, I worked twenty hours per week at Jacobs. My day consisted of driving the brutal Houston traffic (in my thirteen-year-old car) to morning classes. I'd leave campus around 11:30 for my draftsman job – catching a burger at a drive-thru and eating at the wheel as I drove to work. I'd work 12:30-4:30 at my drafting table, and return back to campus for evening classes. I'd get my reading and homework done at night, prior to crashing around 1AM. It was a hard, disciplined routine that has served me ever since.

Jacobs in Houston was very good to me. Even when the nationwide recession hit in 1983 and their overflowing offices of draftsmen and engineers dwindled to me and a handful of other men, they kept me on - which allowed me to complete my studies. On the other hand, Jacobs in Lakeland was not so kind. They paid the first three semesters of tuition, as promised, but when the recession hit, their checks stopped. And they stopped returning my phone calls. I never said anything to the Houston office about the breach because I didn't want to risk losing my job. So, I paid the tuition myself from my part-time draftsman earnings. I watched every penny. I didn't bother to ask family for any help; things were tough in Florida too.

As I was preparing to graduate from UH, with honors, in May 1984, I let Jacobs' Houston office know that I had been accepted for the Master's program at the University of Notre Dame with a full scholarship and stipend. Notre Dame was actually going to pay me to study a subject I had come to love. No more working and studying; just studying. I was on Easy Street.

A few days later, the senior manager asked me to his office. He had been very good to me during the lean years. He said, "Lance, congratulations. I understand you've been accepted to Notre Dame. But what about the two years of employment you promised?" I replied, "You mean the two years I promised in exchange for the Lakeland office paying my tuition? Well, they stopped paying me two years ago and wouldn't return my calls. That agreement was voided by them." The look on his face was one of incredulity. His exact response was, "Those dumb bastards." He wished me all the best and made me promise to call him when I finished at Notre Dame. He'd hire me.

I did actually return to the Lakeland office, when nearing graduation at Notre Dame, and interview for a position there. All of the people I had known were gone. The early eighties recession hit Florida hard. The office was a ghost town. Despite the bad treatment, I returned for the interview because I still had my goal to return home as a chemical engineer to the phosphate industry.

During the interview, a nice beleaguered senior engineer looked at my resume, and asked, "So, Lance, why do you want to come here?" I gave him my pat answer of wanting to work in the phosphate industry. He patiently listened and said, "Son, you're too talented to work in this dying industry. Only the old guys like me, with no options, are hanging around. I'll be happy to give you a job but you can do anything you want. Go do something else." And just like Nana, he changed my destiny in a sentence.

That advice set me on a journey far beyond Florida for the next thirty-five years. It allowed to me to find my wife, Eri, in Tokyo, which led to twenty-one years of blissful marriage and our beautiful daughter, Stephanie. And it enabled me to accomplish things for myself and my family far beyond the simple dream of being a chemical engineer to the phosphate industry. Before she was age five, Stephanie had visited more countries than the number of *counties* I had visited in Florida by the same age. Coldly, that blissful life was interrupted by Eri's sudden death in 2009; and her unexpected death cast me into a new stage of my life, one from which these musings were given birth. But, even after the decades, my life remains impacted by phosphate...

Bone Valley

Phosphate was discovered, by accident, in the Peace River in 1881 by a member of the Army Corps of Engineers, Captain J. Francis LeBaron who was actually looking for fossils – abundant in the Peace River Valley region. When he submitted the black pebbles to the Smithsonian, they were found to be phosphate rock; and the phosphate industry was born in Central Florida.

Growing up in Polk County, we used to hunt for fossils in the abandoned mining areas. Large bones and giant shark teeth made up my fossil collection, as could be similarly found with my fellow Scouts. The fossils we found were the precursors to today's phosphate; late additions to the sediment whose decay had been interrupted by the retreat of Florida's sea line. With the rising and falling of the Earth's oceans, over eons, from the melting and freezing of the ice caps, Florida's width has varied from only ten miles wide at the Florida ridge to many hundreds of miles wider that we know it today. That delicate cycle continues.

With the discovery of phosphate, American Agricultural Chemical Company was formed by a Yankee entrepreneur, Peter Bradley. While early phosphate ore was initially transported by barge down the Peace River to awaiting ships at Charlotte Harbor in Southwest Florida, Bradley saw the efficiencies in rail transport. He envisioned a rail line from Central Florida to a deep water dock at Charlotte Harbor. (Bradley Junction, the sleepy wide spot in the road in Polk County, is named after Peter Bradley and is the junction where the East-West rail line meets the North-South line.) Bradley's vision for connecting the Gulf with Central Florida would impact Kim and me and our families over one hundred years later.

Early Phosphate Transport Barge – Peace River

Bradley set about manifesting his vision with the establishment of a port at the South end of Gasparilla Island, at Boca Grande Pass. Gasparilla Island was a mosquito-infested mangrove jungle at the time, but it did have the benefit of deep water at Boca Grande Pass. Bradley purchased the right of way for his rail line (which would become Seaboard and later CSX) from Central Florida to the "phosphate dock" at Boca Grande. At that dock, large seagoing cargo ships would quickly load phosphate ore straight from the rail cars and return back to sea.

Being a wise entrepreneur, Bradley bought up the mosquito breeding grounds around his right of way and had it platted.

Albert Gilchrist (coincidentally an engineer and citrus man), who would later be governor, surveyed and laid out the streets and plazas. Development proceeded. The area is now known as Boca Grande – a grand destination for the wealthy.

Bradley built the Gasparilla Inn to house the wealthy Northern guests and leveraged his new rail line to transport not only phosphate but wealthy tourists from the Northeast to the sub-tropical paradise known as Boca Grande, the Tarpon Fishing Capitol of the World. Presidents, dignitaries and, more importantly, National Championship college football coaches now reside and visit there.

It All Comes Back to Snook

While I was training to be an engineer, I was introduced to Chaos Theory – the theory that everything is connected, in ways in which we can never understand. The classic example is the metaphor of the butterfly which flutters its wings in China and that action ultimately results in a hurricane in Florida. To a twenty-year-old student, an esoteric theory makes for an interesting thought experiment but it's not something you dwell on too much when you're in the angst of finals. On the other hand, to a middle-aged Floridian with the benefit of fifty years of hindsight, I have come to realize it is not theory; it is fact. Everything is connected – in ways which we cannot predict. Allow me to prove it to you.

To transport phosphate, Peter Bradley built his rail line from Bone Valley in Central Florida to its terminus at the loading dock in Boca Grande pass. That terminus became known as the "phosphate dock." For decades, until its removal in 1980, this magnificent structure saw the loading of phosphate to cargo ships from around the world. But besides enabling an industry to grow, and fortunes made, the phosphate dock became the hangout to some of the largest Snook you've ever seen.

With a strong outgoing tide, the lazy goliath Snook would lay up in the shade of the dock and the camouflage of the pilings, waiting for supper to come downstream with the ripping current straight into their bucket mouths. The big boys would literally be stacked several layers deep on the right tide. Hence, the phosphate dock became a favorite spot for Snook connoisseurs.

I was introduced to the docks by my stepfather and Snook connoisseur, Vernon Clyatt, in 1977 – who tangentially also introduced me to Palm Island (a fact not discovered till forty years later, but that's another story). An avid Snook fisherman, Vernon came to the area for the fishing and he brought us there a couple of weekends. I was fifteen.

Boca Grande Phosphate Dock, circa 1940

At the dock, the white-hulled center-console boats would be lined up in a neat row, perpendicular to the long edge of the four hundred foot dock, and anchored twenty yards upstream of the docks in the ripping current. The boats were so close, you could almost hand a beer to the boat next to you. On a real strong tide, the trick was to make sure your anchor held and that you didn't get carried back into the pilings; no real mortal danger because you could always motor your way out but utter embarrassment to the weekend admiral who would be in full view of all the other weekend skippers.

The fishing technique was always the same – live pinfish; Snook's absolute favorite meal. Brian and I would catch the pinfish, with cut-up shrimp on hook and line, over some grass flats. The preference was the large ones; about the size of a man's hand. ("Big bait, big fish," as Kim says.) Armed with a dozen pinfish or more, we'd make our way with Vernon to claim our spot in the gauntlet of boats at the phosphate dock. With heavy rods, Vernon would hook the pinfish thru its snout and float one downstream and under the dock. And this is where the real trick begins – not in hanging a Snook but rather in holding on to him. In this skirmish, the Snook has every advantage taught him at the Snook School of Dirty Fighting.

First, the mere physics of the challenge are against you. Connecting you with the fighter is a thin thread of a line. Yes, it may be eighty-pound test line, but compare that to a twenty- to thirty-pound Snook, with the additional force and pulling power of his muscles and that of the rip current. So you lose some to break-off. Then, there's their razor gills which can slice a line. So you lose some to slice-off. Then, there's the barnacle-infested pilings which Mr. Snooky is expert at rubbing that thin thread of line against, which you lose to cut-off. Either way, the odds are at least 10:1 in favor of Snooky.

That's the excitement and why men (and women) returned to the phosphate dock. When a boat did manage to land a Snook, the cheers from all boats went up and everyone popped a new beer – kinda like a redneck twenty-one gun salute. It was Miller time.

Thanks to Chaos Theory, that phosphate dock and rail line would ultimately lead me to my home on Palm Island forty years later...

Foxes

Kim's parents, Nell and Ray Fox, have been married for over sixty years. Originally from Tennessee (like Papa Edwards), Nell and Ray eloped to be married outside of the state when Nell was sixteen (she was too young to be married in Tennessee). Ray was twenty. Work opportunities brought them to Florida, and ultimately Lakeland, where they raised a family of Foxes: Kevin, then Kim and finally Keith.

Whereas I've spoken about self-made men, I need to point out that the attribute "self-made" is not reserved for the male sex. It includes the fairer sex as well. Nell is my Exhibit A. A sharp woman, Nell was a very successful realtor in Central Florida; in fact, her Coldwell Banker realty business and office was recognized repeatedly as one of the most productive Coldwell Banker offices in the nation. You don't want to go up against Nell in a negotiation. She has a cool, disarming style to her. A gentle lady, she has the nicest way of practically telling someone, "You're an idiot if you think I'm going to agree to that. Here's how it's going to go down" (my words).

Nell Fox, Kim Fox Edwards, Riley, Ray Fox, 2018

Ray is a railroad man of four decades. I suppose he's ridden every line in the state at one time or another – hauling not people but materials and phosphate. He's been an observer of native Old Florida which I envy – seeing the state's natural wilderness from the view of his cab, dragging a long line of cars across the land not yet tarnished by man's encroachment. It was Ray's phosphate rail line connection and his love of fishing which ultimately connected Kim and me at Palm Island. Remember the butterfly fluttering its wings in China? Ray is my butterfly here.

While Kim was growing up, Nell worked during the day and Ray often worked the nights so they were indeed like two trains passing in the night. Without the benefit of cell phones or answering machines, Nell and Ray communicated by notes left on the fridge. They were two hardworking parents doing all they could for their young family. And, as a young family, one of the Fox's favorite destinations, when they could schedule it, was the Englewood and Boca Grande area. Ray was introduced to the area by virtue of his train hauls to the phosphate dock, where he was forever lured by Snook.

Ray is the most accomplished Snook fisherman I know. He's the Snook Whisperer. I've literally seen him call up Snook to his ankles by teasing them with "greenbacks" (live sardines). I came up to him one afternoon with his Snook gathered around, as if school was in session. Ray baited a hook with a greenback and handed me a pole. "Throw it right there," as he pointed to a spot next to the mangroves ten yards away. As soon as the greenback hit the water, Boom! Snook on. I wrestled the yearling to the beach; held him up for examination and let him go (only to be devoured moments later by a thousand-pound porpoise who swished into the knee-deep water after that unsuspecting Snook. Ray's porpoises know his fishing prowess as well and they had become quite the poachers).

From his initial discovery of the area, Ray caught the Snook bug and the family trips to Englewood increased in frequency. Once all of the kids had flown the coop, Ray and Nell decided it was time to up their game with a beachside condo. They drove up and down the Englewood-Placida strip seeking the perfect place. Ray wanted something with easy access to fishing; Nell wanted a view of the beautiful Gulf sunsets. They settled on their top pick at a little known place called Palm Island. Nell, the seasoned real estate negotiator, put in her somewhat low bid, with instructions to her agent to make an offer on their second choice if her first offer was not accepted (with a wink added, I'm sure, to communicate to the seller that she was bidding on two properties).

Ray was silent on the two-hour drive back to Lakeland from their property tours, sure that they had lost the chance for their first choice. "I thought we came down here to buy a condo," he grumbled. "We just did," replied Nell confidently. And guess what... the seller accepted Nell's first offer and the Fox's twenty-five year connection to Palm Island began. Later, when events in my life dictated a new stage for me and a return to Florida, I reconnected with Kim. And she introduced me to Palm Island. I sit here now typing this manuscript from our beach home overlooking the Gulf, on Palm Island.

Ray Fox, The Snook Whisperer. Palm Island, 2018

I marvel at the connections: the apparently incongruous sequence of events over more than one hundred years connecting phosphate to Boca Grande to Snook to rail to Kim to me. Never would I have guessed that I would end up here. I can see it now in hindsight but we can't know in advance how the butterfly fluttering its wings will impact us. Yet, it will. Because here's what I've learned…

Everything is connected.

The Back Story

For additional background information, audio and video interviews and/or the unpublished photos for this chapter, visit:

BONUS: The Back Story – Bone Valley Gold
http://www.AISBbook.com/Ch03

Chapter 4

The Grande Dame

Up to this point, I've concentrated mostly on the men of Old Florida - the self-made men. Now it's time to focus on the fairer, but tougher, sex – the women of Old Florida.

It's said that, "Behind every successful man, there's a good woman." Well, that is certainly true but that statement does not give due credit to women. Look at any strong clan and you'll find a strong woman, sometimes despite the man. I was blessed to be born into a clan that was full of strong women. But no woman exemplified the Old Florida spirit, with grace and eloquence, like my paternal grandmother, Theodora "Pat" Viola Wood (Edwards) Safford. She was unique. My stepfather, Jeff Wiley, crowned her, "The Grande Dame." I called her Nana.

Nana was queen over the Edwards clan for seventy-five years. Whereas my great-grandmother, Granny Edwards, could be scary in her toughness; Nana was all wise and loving in hers. When some of the Edwards men would, in Nana's words, "lose their minds," she single-handedly held the clan together. There was never any question of who really ruled the roost in the Edwards family – male or female. And, in the process, she instilled in me my love and respect for Old Florida, the land and everything living in it.

Nana lived a full life, dying at age ninety-five in 2013. As I did at Dad's funeral, I spoke about this amazing woman – feeling qualified as an observer and disciple of hers for fifty years. In that eulogy, I explained how this lady was actually three personas in one. And I think that three-persona analogy is my best method for conveying the majesty and spirit of The Grande Dame of Old Florida.

Theodora Viola

Nana's birth name was Theodora Viola Wood. Now there's a very unique name – Theodora Viola - a very proper New England type of name, reflecting her Connecticut birth home. (As an aside… when I was born, Nana suggested that Mom and Dad name me, her first grandchild, Theodore, after her Theodora. My maternal grandfather, Papa Porter, a man known to candidly speak whatever was on his mind and who knew Theodora simply as "Pat", protested, "Theodore? Theodore? What kind of name is Theodore?" Thankfully they settled on Lance.)

Theodora was born in New Haven, Connecticut and grew up as a single child. In the 1920's land boom of Florida, her father moved their small family from New Haven to Lakeland where he chased his fortune as a builder. Eight-year-old Theodora arrived in Florida in 1926. She spent the next eighty-seven years making the point that she was not a Yankee.

The image of Theodora that has always stood out for me is the wedding picture from Mom and Dad's wedding in 1959. Theodora is standing proud and erect, next to the happy couple. She's wearing an elegant gown, an absolutely stunning display of a woman. She appears as if she had just stepped out of Vogue magazine, subtly revealing her New England heritage.

Theodora and Grandpa (Tillis Edwards)
Mom and Dad's Wedding, 1959

Theodora loved the finer things in life. Across the decades, Theodora established, supported and/or served as President of many organizations, societies and clubs that served her adopted home's cultural, health and spiritual needs. Much of the history of Theodora is entwined in the development of Lakeland.

Theodora is the woman with that great mind who graduated as salutatorian of her class at Lakeland High School. At Florida Southern College in Lakeland, she was the first woman on the college debate team. (She chose Florida Southern simply as the only financial option to a Depression-ravaged family of 1937; her father, the builder, bartered Theodora's tuition in exchange for his services in building the college.)

Theodora was a deep thinker with uncanny wisdom and insights into life and the human condition. And she often shared those insights and wisdom in the form of her poems. That was Theodora.

Pat

Despite her formal name, Theodora was known to her friends as simply "Pat." In her 1936 Lakeland High School Yearbook, there are six words printed to describe Pat Wood: "Gracious and kind, a perfect lady." Now, that description would be enough for a lifetime for most but Nana was much more than that.

The image of Pat that stands out for me is the photo of her hanging on the wall in the Florida room of her old Lakeland homestead, now Uncle David and Aunt Bonnie's home. Pat is in the Florida scrub, with pine trees in the background. She's wearing a hunting vest and she's again standing proudly with a beaming smile and perfect hair. But this time, she has the butt of a 16-gauge shotgun hitched to her hip with the barrel pointing in the air. This is the lady of Old Florida.

Pat - Quail Hunting in Florida Scrub, 1972

Beyond Old Florida, she would accompany Grandpa on hunting expeditions to Canada's remote Yukon territory. They'd camp and travel in the wilderness on horseback, searching for trophy mountain sheep and grizzly bear. Beyond her penchant for hunting and fishing, she was the first lady golfer at Lakeland's Lone Palm Golf Club to shoot a hole-in-one. For Lakeland, at least, she was quite the Renaissance Woman.

Pat loved life and everything living. She studied biology and even held early dreams of becoming a doctor. Pat wanted to constantly partake in the never ending life cycle of seed, growth, blossom and restart. Pat loved to plant a seed, nurture it and help it bloom to its absolute fullest potential. She did this with countless varieties of flowers in her yard for decades. And even when she ultimately moved to a condo and the Condo Association rules forbade her from planting in her own yard, she planted seeds in pots in her garage just so she could continue to be part of that cycle. And she became known in the neighborhood as "the little lady with the plants in her garage."

Pat combined her *love for life* with Theodora's *love for the finer things* by transforming raw plants and flowers into abstract floral arrangements which revealed her insights into the human condition. Pat could see the beauty and potential in just about anything.

Ultimately, she would become certified as a Master Judge of Flower Shows by the National Association of State Garden Clubs and travel internationally to Colombia judging others' creative floral work and expressions.

I think it was her love for life and her penchant for cycles and rhythm – *with a beginning, a peak and an end* - that led to her passion for the beach, specifically Anna Maria Island.

Few people know this but Pat was so in-sync with the cycle and rhythm of the tides that, up until two weeks prior to her death, you could ask her on any given day, "Nana, when are the tides at Anna Maria today?"

And, from memory, she would immediately tell you to the minute the times for the low and high tides that day. I think it was the first thing she checked in the Lakeland Ledger newspaper each morning.

Pat also loved her church. For 87 years, she supported All Saints Episcopal Church of Lakeland and saw all her children, grandchildren and great-grandchildren baptized there; me in 1961; my daughter, Stephanie, in 1990.

That was Pat.

Five Generations of Edwards, 1990
Front: Granny & Stephanie
Back: Grandpa & Nana, Lance & Eri, Mom & Dad

Now, my brother, Brian, makes this point. "If you knew her as Pat or Theodora or Mrs. Edwards or Mrs. Safford, you were blessed. If you knew her as Nana, you were one of the luckiest people on the face of the Earth."

Which leads us to the third persona of Nana, or "Kooky Nana" which she proudly self-proclaimed. And that's how her family knew her.

Nana

The best image of Nana, for me, is taken from cousin Jay Edwards' film, "Stomp! Shout! Scream!" - the Skunk Ape film I introduced in Chapter 3.   Nana has a cameo in the movie which was shot at her beloved Anna Maria Island in 2003 – ten years before her passing. But it's not a scene from the final movie which is my favorite, but a scene from the outtakes that impressed me.

In the outtake scene, Nana is wearing this floppy beach hat and giant sunglasses; and she's seated on the beach in a beach chair. She's holding her hat against the wind with one hand and a 1960's replica transistor radio to her ear with the other hand.   You can hear Jay – behind camera - giving direction to someone in the background.   The next thing you know... Nana is giving Jay direction on how to shoot the scene.   And that's Nana...   always available to give direction to the director.

Nana on set of Stomp! Shout! Scream!
Anna Maria Island, 2003

The movie is a merger of genres: monster movie meets 1960's beach music rock and roll.   Cousin Jay named the characters of the story after his grandparents, on both sides.   From the Edwards' side, Tillis (Grandpa's name) is the sheriff of the 1960's Gulf-side town being terrorized by a rogue Skunk Ape, which washed in from the Everglades on a jumble of branches, following a hurricane. The all-woman rock and roll band is named The Violas (Nana's middle name) and the lead singer is Theodora (Nana's official first name). *Spoiler Alert*: The character, Theodora, contracts syphilis. (It's okay. She still gets the man in the end.) It's a kooky movie, perfect for Kooky Nana, who was also one of the financial backers; which leads to my next point...

Nana loved her family. And she brought all three personas to bear when it came to raising her family. She wanted the best in life for each of us. We were each a seed that deserved her nurturing so that we could each reach our full potential – which she could uniquely see.

You knew that Nana was always thinking of you and took an interest in *every detail* of your life. *And I mean every detail*. And she was not afraid to ask you about it. For example, you knew that if you introduced someone to Nana who you were romantically interested in, the newcomer could immediately expect a question from Nana about your sex life. Seriously... to Nana, that was just part of the living process.

There is so much more about Nana that we miss beyond *her probing questions* – the smell of her soup on the stove; the yoo-hoo she shouted when you entered her always-unlocked back door, the phone calls, the letters, the advice, and most of all her genuine caring and love.

But it was her time. And Nana was prepared.

She left us detailed written instructions on what to do when she passed. Written in 1988, twenty five years prior to her death, her hand-written plan included her obituary, her choice of hymns, and her selected reading from Corinthians ("The seed you sow does not come to life unless it has first died"). It was her last direction.

Finally, in her written instructions, she wrote "This is My Belief: We never really die, but are born in another form" - just like the seed in Corinthians. She wanted that passage emphasized at her final farewell. And I conveyed that from the pulpit as my final dutiful act for her.

Anna Maria Island

Anna Maria Island (known simply as Anna Maria and pronounced by Old Floridians as "Anna Ma-rye-a") is one of the barrier islands that strings along Florida's Gulf Coast from Tampa Bay down to Palm Island and even further South below Charlotte Harbor. Anna Maria is the Northern tip of that chain.

Up until the 1980's, these islands were largely known only to locals like Nana and Grandpa. In fact, Grandpa bought their lot on Anna Maria in 1964 and built their beach house in 1965 – one of the first houses on the island. Grandpa paid $10,000 for the lot – a staggering amount in 1964. Today, that same lot on Anna Maria, undeveloped, fetches seven figures.

My parents introduced me to the island but I inherited my love for it and all natural Florida beaches from Nana; yet another reason I now live on a barrier island. Life is simple at the beach but it's even simpler on barrier islands. Largely protected from the high rise hotel and condo developments which clog Atlantic coast beaches with tourists (like Daytona, Vero and Miami), the Gulf coast barrier islands are Old Florida. There literally is an "island time" on the barrier islands.

A lifelong lover of Anna Maria, my earliest recollections of the beach are of Nana and Grandpa's beach house on Anna Maria overlooking Tampa Bay and the Sunshine Skyway bridge. Nana and Grandpa were in their prime and together they made what would be called a power couple today – at least in their small corner of the universe, Old Florida.

During the summers, Grandpa would spend long weekends at the beach with Nana, flying his private Cessna down from Lakeland to the grass air strip on the island. You see, among his other accomplishments, Grandpa was an expert pilot. During World War II, he was an instructor of British fighter pilots, at Lodwick Field in Lakeland. Flying Stearman biplanes, he would train the green students how to fly.

As a boy, Grandpa would regale me with his flight stories, like the time he was teaching a flight student how to recover from a nose dive in the Stearman. In the midst of the dive, the student froze up with a death grip on the stick, which Grandpa could not break from his instructor's stick in the rear. The plane was accelerating to the Earth and Grandpa could not outmuscle the terrified student pilot. Sitting on the edge of my seat, I asked my grandfather, "What did you do?" He explained, "Well, I just started talking calmly to him over the headset, explaining what a fine job he was doing. Eventually, he calmed down and released the stick in time for me to recover control before we plowed into the dirt." "Is that all you did," I asked. "No," replied Grandpa. "When we got out of the plane, I knocked him on his ass for scaring me like that." Lesson over.

Another time, he explained in 1969 how he would sometimes fly his Cessna under the span of the Sunshine Skyway bridge. (In 1980, that same span would collapse into the bay one foggy morning when an errant cargo ship rammed into the steel pillars anchoring the bridge's infrastructure to the bed of the bay. Besides the ship captain not being able to see the bridge's columns in the fog, neither could the car drivers on the bridge above see more than a few feet in front of them. Several cars, including a Greyhound bus, could not see the missing span at the top of the bridge and blindly drove their vehicles off of the bridge into the bay waters, 150 feet below. Eventually, the fog lifted enough for a driver to see and brake his car just before he, himself, went over the edge. He stopped his car at the ragged edge of the collapsed 1,200 foot span and leaped out to stop any further cars from driving off the bridge; but not before thirty five people drove to their deaths that horrific morning.)

Sunshine Skyway Bridge Disaster, 1980

Over the span of my first twenty years, I can't imagine how many trips I made to Anna Maria, first with family and then with high school friends who loved the Old Florida place as much as I. My best friend, Paul Templin, and I spent practically every weekend of every Summer in our late teen years on the white beaches of Bean Point philosophizing on life; with the vast aqua marine waters of the Gulf and the backdrop of the Australian pines. In three Summers on those beaches, I'm confident I received a lifetime of sun radiation, which I take into account today. To see me today on a boat in the Gulf, you'd think you were witnessing a mummy at the helm.

It was at Anna Maria that Nana demonstrated to me her love of life and the natural cycle of all things living. She was a conservator before it became a fad but not the radical tree-hugging type of conservator. She simply understood that everything is connected and we truly reap what we sow. She understood the Butterfly Theory of Chaos I explained in Chapter 3 without knowing there was such a theory. She simply was that in tune with nature.

As a national judge of floral arrangements, she would always amaze me at how she could interpret life in floral arrangements. She'd look at a looping of flowers and branches in a vase and explain to me how it was symbolic of the cycle of life. As a seven-year-old, I'd respectfully listen but couldn't begin to fathom what she meant. Yet, fifty years later, I remember those explanations and finally came to appreciate what she intuitively knew.

It was that appreciation for life and study which led her to return to college in her fifties, following her divorce from Grandpa, to pursue her earlier desire to become a doctor. At age fifty something, she found herself in biology class with the teenagers. (Whereas her first college stint was interrupted by her marriage to Grandpa, this mid-life college term would similarly be interrupted by her marriage to Robert Safford. Not to be deterred, Nana would return to college yet again, in her eighties, after Bob's passing. Frankly, she should have been the one teaching.)

Living off the Bay

At Anna Maria, Nana introduced young Brian and me to clamming, while Grandpa demonstrated his mastery of how to hunt mullet – all within seventy-five yards of the back of their beach house. Within that short radius of water, we learned our connection with the sea and its bounty.

Buried beneath the sand of Tampa Bay, Nana taught us to find clams: hard clams and sunrays (sunrays are named for their image of the sun's ray's on its shell; just like sunset over the Gulf). Clamming is a simple process. The preparation and cooking is the hard work. Fortunately, Brian and I were only tasked with the fun part - finding them.

Beginning at low tide, when the bay withdraws and exposes the sand bars, you walk amongst the wet sand of these temporary islands to locate the clam holes; holes in the sand about the diameter of your pen tip. Using your official clam prober (a long flat-headed screw driver), you stick the probe eight inches down the hole until you tap something hard. Eureka. That's the clam's shell. Next, armed with your extractor (a garden hand-shovel), you dig and harvest your catch. You're looking for the big clams, the ones at least as big as your hand.

Brian and I could have gone on for hours (or until the tide came back in) filling buckets of clams but Nana always made sure we didn't take more clams than we could eat. She respected the balance and told us so. "We can always come back for more as long as we don't take too many," she'd say.   I suppose those were my first lessons on respecting the land and Mother Nature.

Once procured, the next steps were the arduous ones. Brian and I would usually disappear for this part, only to reappear when we heard Nana call out "Yoo hoo, the chowder is ready."   But, in the interim, she would place the clams in a large bucket of fresh water so that the clams could "spit." "Spitting" is the clam's process of ejecting all of the sand within its shell.   Unless you want gritty chowder, it's a critical step in the preparation process. Taking several hours, you'd monitor their "spitting" progress by the accumulation of sand in the bottom of the bucket. The end was signaled when the clams expired and finally opened their shells. The fact that clams can "spit" was a fascinating discovery to a five-year-old.

Once "spitted," Nana would scoop the white muscle out of the opened clams and place the husk of meat in a stewing pot of vegetables, special seasonings and other secret ingredients to conjure up a clam chowder that beats anything in New England. Nana's chowder was the real deal.

Sunray Clam Shell

Whereas low tide found Nana clamming on the bars behind their house, high tide found Grandpa hunting the same territory – with a cast net. This time the prey was mullet – a sixteen-inch, blunt nosed, fish. A good eating fish, what makes mullet unique is that they are impossible to catch by traditional bait and hook. Why? Because mullet only eat decaying leaves and algae. Try bait-hooking a leaf; or algae. It's impossible. So you use a cast net.

A cast net is a ten to thirteen-foot diameter circular net which you throw with the same motion as if you were throwing a bale of hay off the back of a pickup truck; except with a lot more grace. It takes two hands, lots of coordination, and upper body strength.

Throwing a cast net is definitely an art form. Do it wrong and you end up with a tangled pile of net at the bottom of the bay. Done properly, it is ballet in motion. To call it ballet is maybe a little over the top but it's quite the athletic endeavor to execute a precise net toss - as measured by the perfection of the net's circular form, at its zenith. And as with everything Grandpa pursued, he was a maestro at it. In fact, he had his nets handmade because he couldn't buy the large thirteen-foot nets in the store. And, he demanded the biggest and best of everything. (I still have his favorite net at the house.)

Grandpa would do his mullet hunting late in the afternoon when the wind had laid down and the water was still; the sun's rays were stretching long and low on the horizon, just as they look on the shell of a sunray clam. He'd quietly and slowly wade thru the water, waist deep, seeking signs of mullet near the surface. Mullet are schooling fish and the objective is to bag a big bounty with a single cast of your net.

On a flat surface, a school of swimming mullet leave a distinctive V-patterned wake, much like the V-shape of flocking mallards. With his abundant net gathered up in both hands and cocked over his left arm, he'd patiently wait in position until the mullet approached within his reach – within the ambush zone. Then, with a sweeping toss, he'd cast the net out in an expanding circumference over the mullet. The lead weights of the net would crash the circular pattern of nylon violently against the surface and a dozen or more mullet were trapped. Slowly, he'd pull the taut line in and gather the net up into a large sock, full of fish. To see a master at work, like my grandfather, was a joy. It was as much Old Florida as the scene of Dewey George rowing us along the mangroves in the Ten Thousand Islands.

And like Nana's clams, Grandpa's mullet were a delicacy; prepared in a special way. In fact, prepared the only way you can cook mullet - you smoke them. Smoking is the process of curing mullet fillets thru hours of exposure to low heat and smoke.

Grandpa used a special smoking device - the shell of a broken-down Frigidaire refrigerator. To Nana's chagrin, he kept this old rusted appliance in front of their lovely Florida beach home, in sight of the road. On this point, Grandpa was deaf to her protests. An old refrigerator is the tried-and-true absolute best vehicle for smoking mullet. The shelves make perfect racks for stacking the fillets. Plus you're afforded easy access by the wide-opening side door. And as far as the heat source, you simply remove the bottom of the appliance and create a fire pit where you stoke wood and charcoal. Finally, you cut holes in the top of the old gal and you've got yourself a world class smoker. All that's left is the mullet and the choice of wood for the fire. Grandpa's favorite was citrus wood. Readily abundant to a citrus man, citrus wood provides a unique smoked taste to the cured fillets.

Needless to say, when you came to Grandpa and Nana's beach house, you were always in for a culinary treat; a meal that you can't buy in the finest five-star restaurants. From Houston to Tokyo to Paris, I've never found any dining establishment that could match Nana's chowder or Grandpa's mullet, all harvested from the bay.

Boats, Beaches and Bars

For my first two decades, I spent a large portion of each summer at either Anna Maria or its neighboring barrier island, Longboat Key. Unknown to the tourists, these two Gulf coast islands not only afford visitors some isolation, they also host the whitest sand beaches found anywhere. Even the beaches of my own Palm Island cannot compare to the sugar-like sand of these upper islands.

As a youngster, my recollections were of beach time and pool time, interrupted by lunch - followed by more beach time and pool time. Sun was the enemy and I was bad about neglecting Mom's urgencies for sun screen or wearing a white t-shirt as protection. One young Summer, my exposure was so bad, I actually developed second-degree burns on my shoulders with large blisters. No one could tell me anything. The place was paradise to me.

Water time was interrupted by fishing or clamming - or boating. Boats were a large part of life at the beach. Grandpa seemed to have a new boat each Summer. He traded boats like he traded cars. When it was time for an oil change, he got a new car. I suppose each year when kingfish season opened, he felt it was time for a new boat. These beach experiences, combined with our Glades trips and our waterskiing jaunts on the lakes of Lakeland, secured boats as a fixture of life in Old Florida.

There's total freedom with a boat. It's just you and your closest friends and family amidst the natural beauty of Florida. A boat is your escape vehicle from the hustle and bustle. Boats afforded me the joy of initially discovering, and later revealing to family and friends, parts of Florida largely unknown to most.

Outside of basic safe navigation practices, you have few rules with boats, certainly much fewer than cars. And with the exception of the intercostal waterway, there are no speed limits. You can push the throttle to its stops and enjoy the sensation of the motor singing and the wind blasting you in the face. You are free of the limitations of lanes or highways; you have the entire lake or bay or Gulf. You can go practically anywhere you want - as long as you don't run aground on a bar. Speaking of bars, that reminds me of the story Dad used to tell of the harbor pilot at Tampa Bay...

A harbor pilot is the local navigation expert who boats out to the approaching cargo ships and boards the vessel to guide the captain into port. The Tampa Bay pilot had been fetched to the bridge of a large cargo ship on its approach to the bay – a bay known for its sand bars. As the captain's first time to the port in Tampa, he was a little nervous about making his way in. So, he turned to the newly arrived pilot and asked, "So, you know where the sand bars are, do you?" The pilot turned to him blank-faced and said, "No sir. I don't." Even more nervous now, the captain snapped back, "Then how the hell are you going to guide my ship in if you don't know where the bars are?" The pilot answered simply, "Because I know where they ain't."

Back to my boat stories...

Sometime in 1970, Grandpa purchased a new style of boat – an *unsinkable* boat. Built by Aquasport, this fiberglass boat featured a new design in recreational hulls: interior foam panels and a double hull. The sealed hull below the water line was like a giant pontoon that aided the boat's natural floatation. The open, upper hull, with its center console, served as the deck – just like a normal boat. But, to my wonder as a child, the upper hull actually had holes in the back that allowed water to drain out of the boat (or come in if everyone stood in the back). I couldn't imagine how a boat with holes in it could not sink. But, float it did. Later, the Mako line adopted the design and other manufacturers followed. And whereas you can't sink an Aquasport or a Mako, you can damn sure flood one when the lower hull plug pops out – as Paul Templin and I discovered in Tampa Bay one Saturday afternoon.

To round out the boating stories, I have to conclude with a story of near calamity that turned out funny. Sometime in the 1970's, Grandpa and three of his best buddies decided to boat from Miami over to the Bahamas – just as a fun "get away from the wives" kind of trip. Admittedly, at only ninety miles, it's not a Ferdinand Magellan circumnavigation of the globe type of cruise but nevertheless it's a nice clip for a smallish cabin cruiser. Somewhere along the way, the boat sprung a large leak (this was not the unsinkable style of boat). They were able to get an S.O.S. call off to the Coast Guard prior to the boat actually sinking.

By luck, they were within swimming distance of a large navigational buoy, known commonly among the local mariners as the "Susan Buoy." With their distress call, they provided their exact location as the "Susan Buoy." Fortunately, it would just be a matter of time until the men were picked up. Knowing they would not be arriving to the Bahamas and their wives would become concerned when they didn't hear from them, the men asked the Coast Guard to relay their situation to the women folk at home. The Coast Guard agreed.

Unfortunately, the message was scrambled along the way. A new and confused cadet at the Coast Guard radio shack relayed the men's status to their wives as follows, *"Your husband's boat has sunk between Miami and Nassau. The Coast Guard is in route. All of the party are safe and fine. They are with a Ms. Susan Buoy."* Needless to say, each woman's initial feelings of horror from the possibility of losing her husband were fleeting. "Leave the bastard out there," I suspect were the replies.

Red Tide

Nana instilled in me her appreciation for life at the beach. And as I learned later, she believed all of life was a cycle. That rhythm of life was revealed to her in numerous ways; for example, the cycle of the seed to the tree, back to the acorn. It was also revealed in the ebb and flow of the daily tides. As I previously shared, Nana could tell you the times for low tide and high tide at Anna Maria on any given day, whether she was at the beach or not.

One such rhythm which we'd suffer through every couple of years at Anna Maria was a salt water algae bloom, known as red tide. Without warning, red tide would arrive and kill fish, massively. When red tide struck, the beaches were littered with hundreds and hundreds of dead fish; mostly mullet, catfish, and pinfish. The combination of dead fish and Florida sun culminated in a stench that drove you from the beach. You wanted to be upwind of the beach during a red tide kill.

Amazingly, little was known then (and now) what caused it, let alone how to prevent it, or exactly how it killed fish. Non-scientific conventional wisdom amongst the old-timer fishermen was that red tide clogged the gills and the fish strangled to death; the algae did not affect the meat.

Reports of something like red tide can be found in the records of the Spanish explorers of the sixteenth century. Yet, after four centuries, no one could explain it. It hit and after a week or two, it went away. Not to return for two or three years. Nana explained it to me as one of life's rhythms. I didn't think much about red tide again for four or five decades until dead porpoises, sea turtles and manatees started rolling up on our beach at Palm Island in the Summer of 2018. But I'll save that discussion for the final chapter.

Departing on the Morning Tide

The Grande Dame - Theodora, Pat and the lady I knew as Nana - died early on a Tuesday morning in 2013. She lived a full life and, I believe, departed with few regrets. During her last week, she was in palliative care at the hospital. Brian and I took turns staying with her each day and night. At least one of us was always there around the clock. Uncle David called us the "sentries." Even though she was unconscious, the hospice nurse told me Nana still knew someone was there and that oftentimes, the patient hangs on until the final goodbyes are completed. In Nana's case, it made perfect sense to me. She was far too polite to leave a party without saying all her goodbyes.

Over the last week, all of her extended family from all over the country had come to say their final goodbyes. All had been said. That Monday evening, it was Brian's turn to stay and before I left, I took Nana's hand and whispered to her, "Nana, everyone has been here to say goodbye. It's okay to go home now."

I was up early the next morning preparing myself to head down to the hospital and relieve Brian when he called me from her room, "She's passed."

The nurse placed the time of death at approximately 6:15 AM because that's when she checked her. The time of departure was actually sometime between 5:30 AM and 6:15 AM because those were the times between the two check points.

But, for some reason, that wasn't good enough for me. I needed to know the exact time of Nana's passing. So I checked the newspaper. And low tide at Anna Maria Island on that Tuesday morning was 6:04 AM. The form of Nana, Pat and Theodora all exited this life with the low tide at Anna Maria; it was all part of the cycle. *As It Should Be.*

Nana And Her Brood - Her 90th Birthday Party, 2008

The Back Story

For additional background information, audio and video interviews and/or the unpublished photos for this chapter, visit:

BONUS: The Back Story – The Grande Dame
http://www.AISBbook.com/Ch04

Chapter 5

Lakeland

Although the story, so far, has largely focused on the geographical edges of Florida in outreaches of the state such as the Everglades and the Southwestern Gulf Coast, the story really begins in Central Florida, specifically Lakeland.

At the heart of the citrus, cattle and phosphate industries, that small town (population 50,000) was the epicenter of my universe during my formative years. And the root of my orientation to Old Florida tradition and heritage. When unanticipated mid-life changes were causing my inner voice to whisper, "*It's time for a change*," my first thought was of returning to those roots.

Unless you're from Florida (or a big baseball fan), you've most likely never heard of Lakeland. Its claims to fame are being the winter home of the Detroit Tigers and the site of Florida Southern College, a small liberal arts college best known for its Frank Lloyd Wright architecture.

For decades, Lakeland boasted its position as the Citrus Capitol of the World; with more citrus produced in its county, alone, than all of California. Today, with the citrus groves largely replaced by tract homes and mobile home parks, Lakeland boasts its swans, which originally were gifts from Queen Elizabeth, back in 1957.

Downtown Lakeland and its Signature Swans
1948 Postcard (Mom's Collection)

Centered between Tampa to the West and Orlando to the East, Lakeland has really morphed into the continuum of development between those two cities. That area draws attention during national elections as the "I-4 Corridor" – that bastion of conservative voters, known as "Dixiecrats" when I was growing up; since then converted to die-hard Republicans.

From our Florida cracker heritage, native Lakelanders value self-reliance, self-respect, hard work and all things American; especially the constitution. We say "yes sir" and "yes ma'am" no matter our age. We honor traditions and chivalrous behavior. We stand for the National Anthem and applaud the fly-overs at our football games. We respect all things military and have zero patience for those who don't. We love our Florida land and draw energy from the peace of a lake or the serenity of a pine island.

Better Lakeland Than Munnville

Thirty four years after my 4X great-grandfather, James Alderman, became the first white man to ford and settle at the Alafia River in frontier Florida, a Kentuckian named Abraham Munn, purchased eighty acres of land Northeast of Alderman's Ford. Those eighty acres are a scant twenty miles away from the area now known as Alderman's Ford Park. That year was 1882.

In 1884, Munn platted the land for a town and on New Year's Day 1885, the city was incorporated. Of course, it had to have a name and several were considered: Red Bug, Rome City, and the worst of all choices... Munnville. Besides having the vision and courage to incorporate a town in frontier Florida, Mr. Munn had a flare for marketing and (fortunately) opposed the use of Munn in the naming of the city. I can't imagine how the future of the town would have been different if named Munnville – you might as well have called it Dullsville. In fact, I'm sure I wouldn't be here if they had stuck with a dull name like Munnville. Thanks Mr. Munn. I owe you.

The eighty acres Munn platted as the downtown of his new city were surrounded by beautiful lakes: Lake Mirror, Lake Morton, Lake Wire, and Lake Hollingsworth. So the obvious name for Munn's creation was... Lakeland. Over the next four decades, Lakeland found itself in the heart of Florida's nascent citrus, cattle and phosphate industries and the new town flourished. And my family was there.

My great-grandmother, Jessie Tillis Edwards (Granny) lived to be ninety seven years old and I remember that when I'd go to visit her at her farm, she proudly hung on the wall her high school diploma of 1917 from... Lakeland High School. Four generations of Edwards, including me, are proud Dreadnaughts (Lakeland High's mascot of a Navy destroyer).

On the topic of Granny, she was famous for doling out Old Florida wisdom. She had a unique view on everything. After Papa passed, she lived alone and I'd go out to visit her when I was home from college, in the early 1980's. She'd be watching her "shows" and she'd turn off the TV to inquire and hear what was new with me.

In my early twenties at the time, I was apparently showing the signs of early male pattern baldness – something I inherited from her bald husband, Papa. I hadn't really noticed it and no one had ever said anything about it to me – until this visit with Granny. I had just sat down, ready to make chit chat and Granny opens with, "You're losing your hair." I replied, "Do you think so?" She comes back, "I know so." A silent pause hangs in the room. Then came the advice.... "You better get a toupee now while you're young. Then no one will notice." Gee, thanks Granny.

On another trip several years later, Granny was still living at home, in her nineties. Her knees really bothered her and she had a hard time getting around. She was alone at the farm and other than her "shows" she had little to occupy her beyond visits by family. Her son, (Tillis Edwards, my Grandpa) would stop by regularly to let her cook him a meal. And, of course, she'd dole out advice to Grandpa as well. No one was immune. I was following behind one of those trips by Grandpa. During my visit (I was still in my twenties), Granny peppered me with a final piece of advice which has always stuck with me. She said, "Don't grow old." From that day until now, decades later, I still wonder, "What do you do with that advice?"

Granny (Jessie Tillis Edwards), circa 1960's

Manless Land for the Landless Man

By the 1920's, Florida was "settled" and the rush was on for Florida real estate. It's known today as the Florida Land Boom. Hucksters and peddlers of all varieties (legitimate and otherwise) were hawking land to unsuspecting Yankee buyers, each anxious to own a piece of the Sunshine State. In fact, if you visit a Cracker Barrel restaurant in Florida today, look for the 1920's full page newspaper ad they have hanging amongst their nostalgia which advertises Florida real estate, "Manless Land for the Landless Man." During that boom, real estate prices increased, development followed and so was the story with Lakeland.

1920's Florida Land Boom Ad
"Manless Land for the Landless Man"

As a result of the Land Boom, Northerners (in Florida, everyone is a Northerner) migrated into the state and Lakeland; each pursuing a better life. Amongst those Northerners was Nana's family from New Haven, Connecticut (recall The Grande Dame). Her father, my great-grandfather Wood, brought his young family to Lakeland pursuing his riches as a builder. Nana was eight.

Now, to tell the rest of the story and make all the Old Florida connections here, I need to take a step back for a moment...

Back in 1883, around the same time that Mr. Munn was incorporating Lakeland, the first college of the state, South Florida Institute, was founded in Orlando. Over the next two decades, the college moved locations and renamed itself Southern College. In 1922, following fires in other locations, the college moved to its final location, Lakeland. Ultimately, it would settle on the name Florida Southern College. Interestingly, Florida Southern College would connect my family for decades. We simply call it Florida Southern.

Florida Southern College

The grounds were cleared for Florida Southern in Lakeland in 1922. And, guess what, my family was there. President of Florida Southern College, at the ground-breaking, was Rhenus Alderman, grandson to Old Florida pioneer, James Alderman (my 4X great-grandfather). Rhenus is my 3X great-uncle. The connections never cease. (He served from 1914 – 1925.)

President Rhenus Alderman, Right, Clearing The Site for Florida Southern On The Edge Of Lake Hollingsworth in Lakeland, 1922

Great Uncle Rhenus might not have exerted much physical effort in the construction of Florida Southern but my great-grandfather Wood sure did.

You see, the Florida Land Boom ultimately converted to a bust – as all booms do – in the 1920's. Only to be followed by the national stock market bust of 1929. Come 1936, when it's nearing time for young Nana (a graduating Lakeland High School senior) to enter college, times were economically tough in Lakeland. And her father, my great-grandfather Wood, couldn't afford the tuition. I don't imagine too many fathers could.

Not to be denied, great-grandfather Wood arranged a barter of his services in the construction of Florida Southern's Spivey Hall for his daughter's tuition. And Nana goes to college. Hence, I discovered both sides of my family involved in the formation of Florida Southern College. Both Nana and Grandpa attended. More connections.

Brother Brian attended there for a stint between two separate enlistments in the Marine Corps, when he wasn't kicking Saddam Hussein's butt in Operations Desert Shield and Desert Storm. But that's not all…

Mom found her perfect mate there. My late stepfather, Jeff Wiley was a business school professor at Florida Southern for twenty five years, following his twenty year military career with the United States Army. His too-soon death in 2002 left Mom alone and a miracle happened when she married an equally great man, my step father, Duane Hopkins. But get this, Duane was also a business school professor at Florida Southern for twenty five years, following his twenty one year military career with the United States Air Force. What are the odds of that?

The two men each contributed to Florida Southern's MBA program being recognized by Orlando Business Journal as "Best Local School to Get Your MBA;" as well as the college's distinction as #4 on the list of "Best Colleges in the South" by US News and World Report.

It's funny that prior to my research for this book, I never realized all the connections. I just remembered Florida Southern as the place I could drive by on my way home from Lakeland High School and gaze at the bikini-clad co-eds sunbathing on the hill.

Chapel at Florida Southern College
Single Largest Collection of Frank Lloyd Wright Architecture

Lakeland Goes to War

Not unique to Florida but Floridians always answer when their country calls. There is a very strong respect for all things military within Old Florida. It goes to our very roots; deep.

Recall my 3X great-grandfather, Timothy Alderman, served in the Confederate Cow Calvary, to supply Central Florida Cracker cattle to the cause. (As way of Civil War history, the Fall of Vicksburg to Union forces officially cut off the Confederacy from the Mississippi River, one of their two supply lines of beef for the Confederate Army – the other being Florida. This made Central Florida strategic in sourcing cracker cattle to the cause. The Cow Calvary was assembled from Confederate soldiers, like my 3X great-grandfather, to both gather cattle and fend off raiding parties.)

Check out the gem below, which Mom found in her genealogical research. It's Timothy Alderman's Confederate Muster Roll from May 5, 1862...

```
                    (Confederate.)

    A    |    7    |    Fla.

      Timothy  Alderman

    Pvt , Co. B , 7 Reg't Florida Infantry.

Appears on

        Company Muster Roll

of the organization named above,

for          Nov + Dec        , 186 3

Enlisted :

When          May 5        , 186 2,
Where          Alafia  Fla
By whom          Lt  Henderson
Period   3 years a war

Last paid :
By whom    Capt Arnow
To what time      Apr 30      , 1863 .

Present or absent    absent

Remarks: Detailed to drive
cattle in Fla Oct 16, 1863
```

Confederate Muster Roll
Timothy Alderman, Private, Company B of
7th Regiment, Florida Infantry
May 5, 1862 in Alafia, Fla by Lt. Henderson
"Detailed to Drive Cattle in Fla Oct. 16, 1863"

When World War II broke out, both of my grandfathers served that cause. Grandpa Edwards was a military flight instructor for the Lodwick School of Aeronautics at Lodwick Airfield in Lakeland. He logged ten thousand hours teaching basic flying to countless numbers of tenderfoot British fighter pilots.

WWII Pilot Trainers, Lodwick Field, Lakeland, 1943
Grandpa (Tillis Edwards) Fifth from Left

As way of heritage, the Detroit Tigers conduct Spring training in Lakeland today on the site of the old runway at Lodwick Airfield. It's due to this connection to the WWII pilots that Detroit's farm team was called the Lakeland Pilots and later renamed the Flying Tigers. The original plane hangars are still there; it's where we attended "hangar dances" as high school seniors in 1979.

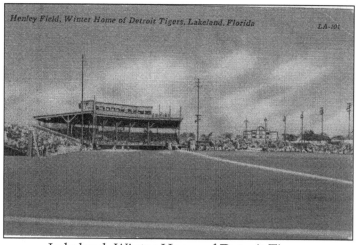

Lakeland, Winter Home of Detroit Tigers
and Farm Team, Lakeland Flying Tigers

Papa Porter, too old to enlist in WWII, applied his mechanical skills to work and worked at Food Machinery Corporation as a foreman to build amphibious tanks, called Water Buffalos (deemed by the army as LTV-1 and LTV-2). Mom, who, was less than five years old at the time, tells the story of how they'd test the tanks in Lake Bonnie, one of Lakeland's many lakes. Papa offered Mom the chance to ride inside, which she refused due to her fear of enclosed spaces. She still remembers that.

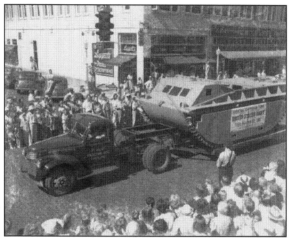

Amphibious Landing Vehicle (Tracked) (LVT-1)
On Display in Lakeland Parade, 1941

Brother Brian came home one day in 1982 to announce to Mom that he had joined the Marine Corps. He went thru boot camp at Parris Island. Although divorced, Mom and Dad, of course, attended his boot camp graduation to discover how their little Brian had, in eight weeks, been transformed into a Marine. But they didn't go alone.

Accompanying them was Bobby Fore (Dad's best friend who joined us on our first Glades trip as youngsters). Bobby was a former (correction inactive) Marine fighter pilot (a Marine will quickly point out that once a Marine, always a Marine; there are no former Marines; just inactive Marines). He insisted on attending the recognition for Brian.

Two Lakeland Marines: Bobby Fore & Brian Edwards
Parris Island Boot Camp Graduation, 1982

I was a college junior at the time of Brian's graduation so the first time I got to see him was during my Christmas break, a few weeks after the commencement. As boys, Brian and I used to scrap quite a bit, the way brothers do. Being older and bigger, I usually came out ahead due to my two year birth advantage and size. Back home and for nostalgic sake, Brian and I started wrestling. I pulled my old maneuver of leveraging my size, expecting him to yield as always. Except this time Brian didn't budge. Not a bit. He allowed me to wear myself out on him for a couple of minutes and then when he bored of the exercise, he tossed me over his shoulder. Me panting. Him grinning. Rematch over. I acknowledged the new champion.

In October 1983, President Reagan unleashed our military on to the small Caribbean island of Grenada to reverse communist forces and rescue American medical students, trapped by the internal strife. The combined power of all military branches quickly made mincemeat of the opposition and rescued all students with not one student harmed. Operation Urgent Fury was quick, decisive and exactly what the American public needed to see; especially following the malaise of the Carter presidency and the failed Iran hostage attempt. We needed a victory; a slam dunk. And our military delivered.

Almost overnight, the view of our military and country was bolstered and President Reagan reminded the nation of who we are. His boldness – in not asking for permission but rather simply issuing the command, "Attack. Now." resonated with Old Floridians. That was the backdrop in October 1983. Now, let me tie this back to Lakeland…

Brian was in the Marines at the time of Grenada but his unit was not called up for the invasion. Instead, he was on training maneuvers in the states when he had an Achilles heel injury and was forced to a cast and crutches, coincident with the time of the Grenada invasion. Within a week of Grenada's successful conclusion, Brian was granted leave to go home and rest his injury.

During his leave in Lakeland, Dad took twenty-year-old Brian to the Foxfire Restaurant, one of the town's finest. A band was performing in the lounge that night and Dad said, "Let's get a drink first, son." Decked out in his Marine dress blues, with cast and crutches, Brian slowly trailed Dad thru the lounge. The band was in full swing but the moment they saw Brian limping across the floor in those dress blues, they stopped their song mid-note and immediately launched into a full chorus of Dixie. The place went crazy in applause. Brian couldn't buy a drink due to the multiple offers to buy one for him. I'm sure Dad accepted some as well. *As It Should Be.*

I share this story to say something that needs to be said…

Confederate Symbols are Innocent

The band didn't launch into the Star Spangled Banner but rather Dixie. Why is that? Because that's how deep the feelings of fighting for a *strong cause* go in Old Florida and the Old South. And that's what the Confederacy represents to the Old South: a fight for a strong cause. Not for slavery but rather for states' rights – a matter that was regrettably left unsettled by the Founding Fathers in the Constitution. Most of the men who fought so desperately in the Civil War didn't even own slaves, including my 3X great-grandfather.

So, despite the fact that the conflict was settled over 150 years ago and there's no living soul from that period, that feeling of fighting for a *strong cause* is in our DNA. We're raised on it as children. We learn of the desperate and suicidal charge by Pickett's brigade across the mile-long wide-open field at Gettysburg; straight into Union cannons. We imagine what that must have been like, to be an eighteen-year-old ordered to "take that hill" and receive cannon fodder at point blank range.

And then we learn of the same heroics at Normandy and have to imagine what it would have been like as an eighteen-year-old in an amphibious landing vehicle ordered to a frontal assault on Normandy beach with German cannons and strongholds in place, with the enemy's advantage of entrenchment and two years of preparation. Another suicidal idea, yet they did it.

The descendants of those Confederate soldiers in Pickett's brigade at Gettysburg were in those landing craft at Normandy and Guadalcanal and Iwo Jima – taking it point blank to the enemy. They were in the Ardennes Forest. They were in Desert Shield and Desert Storm. They were in Korea and Vietnam. They were in Iraq. They are fighting in Afghanistan and untold places today on the land, air and sea, with Old South and Old Florida blood coursing thru their veins. That commitment is what makes us strong.

So why do these men and women do it? Because they are fighting for a strong cause. It's in our DNA. And it's what binds us as Americans. That's the common thread that I believe is difficult to understand for anyone not a descendent of the Old South, which leads to my point that the Confederate symbols are innocent.

There's newly risen controversy over the display of Confederate symbols that have been in place for over one hundred years. Some localities are choosing to remove the statues and monuments. It's very contentious.

In Lakeland, they're debating what to do with the Confederate Monument erected in 1910 at the center of Munn Park to honor Polk County's Confederate war dead. Over one hundred years later, it's now to be moved. It's all absurd. And offensive.

Lakeland's Munn Park and Confederate Monument
1954 Postcard

At the time of this writing, Ft. Myers, Florida is debating what to do with its Robert E. Lee statue. Ft. Myers is the county seat of <u>Lee</u> County – named after Robert E. Lee! And you're going to try and undo that? What's next, changing the name of the county? I'm sorry but give me a break.

Imagine how you'd feel if some group declared that the War Dead Memorial at Normandy or the Iwo Jima monument at Arlington Cemetery was offensive to them and they wanted the monuments removed. You'd feel violated. And wronged. Well, just like we'd fight to protect those monuments, Native Floridians feel the same about protecting the Confederate symbols. It's in our blood. It's our heritage. It's not something to be trifled with.

Now, don't get me wrong. I'm not even hinting at endorsing the neo-conservative fringe groups which seek to bastardize the use of these same symbols into violent acts of hatred and division – whether racial, sexual, anything. They're lunatics.

The symbols are innocent; there's no hate in the monument or flag. Hate comes from humans not objects. We need to address that source. Removing a historical monument doesn't remove hate, in fact it churns it. The symbols are best left alone.

Enough on that. Please save your cards and letters.

Growing Up in Lakeland

For the first seventeen years, up until 1979 when I left for college, Lakeland was the crucible for my formative years. It was a time of moon shots, the nation's bicentennial and the threat of nuclear war. Fast-paced change against a laid-back town with Old Florida traditions that had been in existence for less than one hundred years. Only surpassed by what we see today with the speed of the Internet and social media in changing national mores.

In the first grade (1966), I got to meet John Glenn (the first man to orbit the Earth), who came to our class because his niece was my classmate. I didn't really understand who he was but I remember the event and him. A short three years later, on July 20, 1969, Mom held me (age seven) in front of a black and white TV (with rabbit ears and all) to witness Neal Armstrong set foot on the moon. Each was especially exciting since these space jaunts were originating in my home state. I recall Granny commenting that, born in 1898, she had seen man progress from horse and buggy to the Moon – in just seventy years. Today, the pace is even faster.

At school, our morning ritual was the same for twelve straight years. We'd start with the Pledge of Allegiance, hand to hearts, facing the American flag hanging in each classroom. There was no thought of not participating. Needless to say, there was no kneeling, no peaceful protest. You just did it. It made sense.

The Russians were the enemy and there was the pervasive threat of nuclear war. I was one year old during the Cuban Missile Crisis of 1962 so I don't remember it. But Dad later told me that everyone in Florida was expecting Russian missiles from Cuba to land in Central Florida. The best-selling novel, *Alas Babylon*, had just come out three years earlier - the story about nuclear war at a fictional Florida town named Ft. Repose, based on the actual city of Mount

Dora, Florida – just seventy five miles Northeast of Lakeland. And so Floridians had the feeling of a self-fulfilling prophecy.

In school, we'd practice "tornado drills" which I suspected were a different label for "nuclear attack drills." For the drill, we'd climb under our little desks with our hands over our heads. I had seen on TV the black and white footage of the effects of a nuclear blast and always wondered, "What difference will this flimsy little desk make when the building goes?" Nevertheless, we followed instructions. Tried not to stay too scared.

Duck and Cover Drill, 1960's

But the threat of nuclear war was real to us and constant. Yet we continued life as normal because, even as a youngster, I had been taught to have confidence in our military. We learned of the nation's preparedness with non-stop B-52 bomber coverage, ballistic submarines, land silos, and mobile launchers; with enough combined nuclear firepower to destroy the Earth ten or twenty times over. That was the backdrop of my youth. It was us or the Russians.

When the first Space Shuttle (Columbia) launched and landed in April 1981, I was at Duke as a sophomore. The inaugural mission was NASA's first attempt at reusing a space vehicle; it was an exciting proposition. I remember watching the first landing on TV with the rest of the nation. I was used to the countdown timer on launches for the Apollo shoots but now there was a countdown timer for a landing. And it was displaying the minutes to landing long before Columbia was visible or had even entered the atmosphere.

When she did break thru the clouds, there was a feeling of pride and excitement as the astronauts lined up her flight path to the runway and dropped her landing gear. Jets were accompanying her on either side as she rapidly descended and the countdown ticker slid into single digits. At the exact mark of 00:00, you saw the smoke rise and swirl from the rubber tires as Columbia touched down on the concrete runway. There was silence, broken by, "Columbia has landed."

I was amazed at the precision. Proud to be an American. Even more confident in our technical capabilities. I called Dad to see if he had seen it. After all, he was there when the Russians launched the Space Race with their rink-a-dink Sputnik satellite, way back in 1957. "Dad, did you see the landing?," I asked. He replied, "You bet I did son. And did you see how they knew the exact second she would land? I'd like to see the Russians try that."

Columbia Nails the Landing, 1981

A Boat for Every Household

A view of a Florida map shows that Lakeland doesn't have the highest concentration of lakes in the state but there's a bunch. As a result, a lot of activities are water-bound. In fact, at this point, with so much focus on the Gulf Coast and the Everglades, you'd think we lived on the water. In hindsight, I guess we practically did. It's logical when you live in a place called Lakeland, and on a peninsula.

Besides fishing for Snook on the Gulf, there was freshwater fishing in the lakes for speckled perch, or 'specs as they were commonly known. Thanks to my grandfather, Papa Porter, I've fished nearly every lake in Central Florida in one of his many boats he was always tinkering with. I suppose it's a truism that if you live on a lake, with fish in it, then you must attach the boat trailer to the car and drive fifty miles to fish another lake. At least, that's what Brian and I did with Papa. I can count on one hand the number of times he actually took us fishing on a lake in Lakeland. Instead, his fishing excursions were always at least a thirty minute drive. However, no matter the location, the trips were always eventful. Like I've said, Papa was my fun grandfather.

There is one story with Papa that I can now reveal publicly, forty five years after his death.

In December 1972, I was eleven years old. My teenage cousins, Chris and Tracy Webb, were down from Virginia for their Christmas break to spend the holidays with the entire family. Of course, Papa invited us to go fishing the next morning. After Mama Porter fed us her special creamed chipped beef on toast for breakfast, us three boys and Papa attached his favorite seventeen-foot wooden boat and we all crammed into his red Ford pickup truck and headed for Camp Mack on Lake Kissimmee, East of Lakeland. (Kissimmee is the chain of lakes which originates the water flow South to Lake Okeechobee and ultimately the Everglades – a topic for the final chapter.)

It was December and cold. And about to get colder when Papa got that boat on a plane and we got hit in the face with wind. So we were heavily garbed in coats and all. When we set off from

Camp Mack onto the massive lake, our mission was specs, basically a large bream-like pan fish that's great fried. Papa pulled away from the boat ramp and revved his old Evinrude up to full speed and headed for locations known only to him. Chris, Tracy and I hunkered down behind the wind break of his windshield. That's when it happened...

We had been traveling quite a time and were traversing down one of the fairly narrow canals that connect the Kissimmee chain when Papa temporarily took his eye "off the road," so to speak, and was reaching for something beneath the bow bonnet. We boys were hunkered down below the windshield and weren't paying attention to where we were going. We were all equally notified of our errant trajectory by the shock of the boat hitting the canal embankment and launching the wooden craft up the hill. Recovering from the physical shock of the collision, we quickly caught our wits; the only sound was the noise of the old Evinrude still running at full RPM. (I guess it's true when they say you can't stop an Evinrude. Papa had to switch off the ignition to quiet this bad boy.)

All quiet now, Papa checked us each out. No one was injured. He cleared his throat, mumbled something about it being the boat's fault and said, "Let's get out and check the damage boys." We all climbed over the side to inspect the damage. Wow. The work of an Evinrude is impressive.

The power of the outboard propelled the boat completely clear of the water and fully up the embankment. We were high and dry. The spinning prop had dug a hole in the sand where it sat but fortunately it was fully intact. There was just one problem, a big one...

The ferocity at which the wooden boat struck the sand embankment had knocked a hole in the bow's hull below the water line. The Evinrude survived the impact but the wooden slats of that old boat apparently weren't designed for ramming speed.

Now, you may remember from earlier chapters I said that, short of the machinations of a nuclear submarine, Papa could fix anything. Well, he put that mechanical mind of his to work and came up with a plan. "Gimme your coats boys." We all surrendered our jackets and gave them to Papa. Then he instructed me – the youngest, "Lance, you climb back into the boat and get up in that bow. I want you to wedge these jackets as tight as you can into the hole. Chris, Tracy and I will push the boat back into the water, hop in, and we'll limp home. Oh, one final thing. You stay up-front holding the jackets once I start the motor and let me know if any water comes in."

That was the plan; best there was as he had no materials or tools on board.

I obeyed. I plugged the hole with our cotton jackets and Papa, Chris and Tracy, together, successfully christened the boat back to sea duty. Once afloat, the old Evinrude cranked up as if nothing had happened. And Papa slowly gave her gas and put us underway. Now, the next part of the story is best told from cousin Chris' perspective. So I'm going to share his retelling…

The small bow area I was in was a small cabin, actually a storage area. My little eleven-year-old head was at the point of the bow holding soggy jackets against the breach. My little legs were sticking out the back of the little cabin, in view of Papa, Chris and Tracy. They couldn't see the hole or my head, just my ankles and feet. As Papa increased the gas to gain momentum for the long ride home, water ignored our cotton dam and started to flood in. My warnings started out timidly like, "Papa. Ah… Papa." And as the water volume increased and images of the Titanic came to mind, my little feet and legs started kicking and I shouted out so everyone could hear, "Papa, there's water. Lots of water."

Papa sized up the situation as unworkable and gently beached the bow of the boat on a flat piece of acreage; far gentler than the first landing that morning. After shutting down the motor, Papa revealed Plan B, "Alright boys. That didn't work. So I need to drive back to Lakeland, get some tools and wood from my work shed and return here to fix this boat proper. Chris, you'll go with me. Lance and Tracy, you stay here and guard the boat."

"But Papa," I asked, "How are you going to get back to your truck?" "Simple son, I'll just wave down a passing boat," he easily answered.

And that's what he did. He hailed the next boat that came by and concocted a small fib about how we had the misfortune of hitting a floating log and he needed a ride back to Camp Mack for himself and his grandson. That left just me and Tracy at the boat...

I was eleven and I suppose Tracy was thirteen. Easily bored, we got out of the boat and walked around the scrub land we were beached on; threw sticks, climbed a tree, saw an armadillo - boy stuff.

When we exhausted our standard list of boy stuff and started feeling hungry, we returned to the boat and devoured the boiled eggs that Papa always prepared for our fishing jaunts. Once that was complete, we were now back to being bored. I'm poking around the boat, learning how it works when I found Papa's 22 caliber rifle – and a full box of shells. Bingo. Here's something to do.

Now, stop. Nothing happened.

Like most Florida boys my age, I was already familiar with the safe operation of a single shot 22 rifle. Being from out of state, Tracy was the novice. So I decided to teach him. We set up a target against a tree and commenced target practice for the next hour or so. Interesting how no one ever stopped to inquire about the rifle shots. Actually, in Central Florida, gun shots in the woods are common – especially in December when it's deer season. In any event, we emptied the box of shells not long before Papa and Chris returned with repair material and tools.

As Papa started his marine carpentry repairs, Chris regaled us with Papa's "black parachute drop" into his work shed back home to gather materials... By the time they arrived in Lakeland, it was the middle of the day, and the last thing Papa wanted was to get caught by his daughters (our mothers) or his wife (our grandmother) to explain why he returned home minus two grandsons and one boat. He could spin a tale but spinning this one was even out of his league. So he devised a covert plan for the quiet extraction of his tools.

Papa didn't dare pull up in the driveway with his pickup truck. He'd have to enter from the back.

Papa and Mama's home backed up to a school yard. So, with school conveniently out for the Christmas holidays, Papa drove his pickup across the school yard to the back of his yard, sneaked into his shed and recovered all he needed, with no one knowing the better.

After he finished catching us up on the Lakeland operation, Chris asked, "What have you guys been doing?" "Oh, just some target practice," we answered.

I don't know if Papa overheard the conversation but if he did, he didn't say anything to us. I assume his biggest worry at the time was getting this craft afloat. Otherwise, he would have to resort to Plan C - telling his daughters what happened. I'm sure he would have rather taken a whipping than deal with their motherly wrath.

Of course, Papa could fix anything and he made the boat seaworthy in record time. Except for the obvious patch of two feet of raw wood which stood out against the painted hull, the old craft was good as new. We relaunched her and headed back to Camp Mack. And ultimately made it home safe and sound. However, as we pulled into his driveway in Lakeland, Papa had one final instruction for us, "Now boys. You don't need to tell your mothers about this. Agreed?" "Yes sir," we replied.

And we kept our oath of silence – until a couple years after Papa's passing, when we figured he wouldn't mind. It was another Christmas gathering at Mama's house with the entire family, missing Papa and recounting the tales of this lovable man. It was at the family dinner table that Chris, Tracy and I revealed what happened that cold December day on Lake Kissimmee years prior.

There was shock and horror by Mom and Aunt Pat. Aunt Pat asked, "Why didn't you tell us before?" We replied, "Because Papa asked us not to." And I asked, "Didn't anyone ever notice the patch on the boat parked outside the back door?"

No one actually noticed because Papa was always patching something. Remember what I said, "Papa can fix anything." He was the self-reliant, self-made man – developed out of Old Florida. *As It Should Be.*

Papa (Paul Porter), 1950's

Water Skiing with the Gators

Being surrounded by lakes, water skiing was a natural activity for Lakelanders. Dad was the one who taught us how to ski but Mom was the real water skier in the family. As a teenager, she was a member of the Lakeland Water Ski Club where she did trick skiing exhibits at Lake Hollingsworth.

Mom and Jimbo Allen, 1957

In fact, water skiing (at least trick skiing) was pretty much invented in Polk County, over in Winter Haven – just East of Lakeland. Winter Haven was the home of Cypress Gardens – the mecca for trick skiing. Besides being known for its ski shows on Lake Eloise, Cypress Gardens was known for its all-colorful botanical gardens, its beautiful Southern belles in large hoop skirts and its Florida pool. But here's some trivia for you...

When Cypress Gardens opened in 1936, the Southern belles were not part of the plan, just the gardens and the water skiing. But all innovation comes from desperation and that's what led to Southern belles at Cypress Gardens. In 1940, a freeze killed the lovely flowering vine which greeted guests at the entrance of the attraction. As a dead brown weed, it had the reverse effect, discouraging visitors.

As admissions steadily declined and the Pope Family founders struggled to make ends meet, Mrs. Pope had an aha moment. She gathered the girls in the front office, adorned them in large hoop-skirt dresses and placed them all at the front entrance; strategically placed to block the dead vine. Overnight, sales shot up. And Southern belles in hoop skirts became a fixture at Cypress Gardens.

Over the years, the Southern belles were so thick on the grounds that you had to be diligent you didn't trip over one.

Cypress Gardens Belles

Another fixture of Cypress Gardens was the Florida pool. Built in 1953, it was situated amidst the cypress trees of Lake Eloise and shaped like Florida. It was featured in the 1953 film "Easy to Love," starring Esther Williams and Van Johnson. It had only a small appearance but the pool put Cypress Gardens on the map. But wouldn't you like to know an even more interesting fact about the pool? It was constructed by good friend, Paul Templin's family's business, Templin Construction of Lakeland. *As It Should Be.*

Cypress Gardens' Florida Pool
Built in 1953 by Templin Construction

Cypress Gardens closed in 2009 due to its inability to compete with Disney. The attraction was purchased and converted to Lego Land. The new owners, thankfully, had the foresight to retain the botanical gardens and the Florida Pool. Today, they are open again and you can see firsthand Paul's family's work in Old Florida.

As high school students, Paul and I would drag Dad's boat over to Winter Haven so that we could water ski on Lake Eloise and take in the ski show for free. Boats were allowed to anchor outside of the perimeter of the ski show and watch for free. We always boasted we were going to ski thru the show but talk comes cheap on a boat. Old school friend and fellow skier, Annette Armstrong, would always call our bluff and egg us on but we always folded.

I dragged lots of people out on our skiing jaunts across several lakes while in high school and always a newbie would ask, "Hey, aren't there alligators in this lake?" "Yea," I'd reply. "But shouldn't I be worried about them while I'm wading in the water," they'd counter.

"Na. They won't bother you," was my standard reply. At least, that's what Dad told me when I first asked him while he was teaching me.

The fact is that not once did a gator come within sight of us; at least not my sight. And I've never heard of a gator attacking a water skier. But dogs, that's a different story. Keep your little yappy lap dog away from the banks of a gator-infested lake. A gator will take one of them out in a heartbeat, just to rid the neighborhood of the noise.

Gators are simply part of the landscape in Central Florida. In Lakeland's downtown Lake Mirror, we had an old fella named Blinky, due to him only having one good eye. He lived alone in the lake. Well, I guess he'd get lonely because he'd climb out pretty regularly and walk downtown amongst the pedestrians for an afternoon stroll. His excursions were always in the newspaper. Not once was there an incident or scare.

Blinky On A Stroll in Lakeland

It Never Pays to Laugh at Anyone

Lakeland was a magnet for snow birds in the Winter months. Snow birds was our phrase for the seasonal Northerners who escaped the cold and snow each year from someplace North of the Mason-Dixon line. With its warm weather, citrus groves and laid-back atmosphere, who wouldn't pick Lakeland? Well, if you don't need much entertainment or night life, who wouldn't pick Lakeland? Mostly Lakeland attracted the elder snow birds. The pace there was pretty slow.

I never saw too many of them out on the lakes, skiing. In fact, their chief source of entertainment seemed to be shuffleboard. You know shuffleboard - that athletically demanding sport of scooting a puck down a concrete pad? Lakeland had lots of shuffleboard courts. There was a large set of courts at the Lakeland Shuffleboard Club. And, in fact, courts were pretty much a fixture at every motel in Old Florida.

Lakeland Shuffleboard Club, circa 1940's

Atop the entrance to the Lakeland Shuffleboard Club's courts hung a sign which read, "Enjoy Yourself, It's Later than You Think." As cocky youngsters, we'd see our Northern visitors shuffle boarding regularly and we'd laugh as we drove by. Ha. That's for old folks.

Dad was always quick to remind us, "It never pays to laugh at anyone."

Well, Dad was right. The old folks got the last laugh. Roll the clock forward fifty years. Today, if you look under our home on Palm Island and amidst the stilts, what do you find? That's right, you guessed it. A shuffleboard court. Kim and I had it painted onto the concrete (in Florida Gators' blue and orange). And whenever we gather friends and family, that court is the most popular event. It's a blast. I guess we were wrong about that old folks thing.

Under the house, you'll also find a sign which reads, "Enjoy Yourself, It's Later than You Think." *As It Should Be.*

Lance and Kim's Shuffleboard Court, 2018
At Palm Island. Under the Flags of Florida

You Don't Need A Time Machine

If you want to travel back in time one hundred years, get in your car and take Exit 58 off I-4 in-between Lakeland and Kissimmee. There you'll have a choice; you can head East or head West. If you head West, you'll find Champions Gate and you'll drive into a modern collection of nice new homes and shops, pretty much like any new swanky area in Florida. If you head East, you'll find yourself in Old Florida of one hundred years ago.

When you head East, you're driving along Osceola-Polk Line Road, the county line road separating Polk and Osceola counties. Drive for approximately four miles until you cross the rail road tracks. On your immediate right, you'll see a side road labeled "Old Tampa Highway." Turn right onto it. Drive a short ways until the road turns from asphalt to red brick. At that point, you've arrived. You have stepped back into Old Florida.

That narrow red brick road is the last remnants of the Old Dixie Highway. Built during the 1920's Land Boom, this six-thousand mile long highway connected Michigan to Miami and back to Chicago, catalyzing the population explosion (and the era of roadside attractions like Cypress Gardens). This "modern highway" revolutionized automobile travel for the times. Imagine your Model T bouncing along this narrow road for one-thousand miles filled to the brim with luggage and family. I suppose people were tougher back then. Few today could imagine travel without air conditioning, personal entertainment devices, or reclining seats.

Old Dixie Highway, Built 1920's

As you drive down the old road, you'll find a few houses and trailers on your left but to the right you'll find the original Florida scrub, untouched since this land rose above the sea.

In less than a half-mile, you'll come upon your second prize. It's Marker #2 of the three Polk County welcome markers erected in 1930, at the highway entrances from Osceola, Pasco and Hillsborough counties. I showed you Marker #1 in Chapter 2. So what's so special about Marker #2? Take a look below. Do you notice anything?

Polk County Welcome Marker #2
Notice Anything Unusual?

You're right. On this marker (and this marker only), the word Citrus is misspelled Citurs - on one side, the side facing the road. I suppose they were practicing on this one. Anyway, there it is. Welcome to Old Florida.

Connections

I could go on and on about my formative years in Lakeland but I'll spare you that, maybe save it for a future Volume II. My point is to establish a feeling of Old Florida for you, thru my personal accounts of the land, the people and the times.

Now, a second theme of the book is connections; connections in events, places and people which, although unrealized and unanticipated at the time, conspire to produce the happenings of our life and our world as we know it – something which I discovered by accident and can only be recognized with the benefit of a rear view mirror. After all, isn't that what history is? A backward look upon a seemingly random tapestry of events, places and people to see how they thread their way into the fabric of our lives today.

For example, in the Preface of this book, I've already shared a major connection with my wife, Kim - a connection which began fifty years prior to our marriage when we met in the first grade at Carlton Palmore Elementary School. And the seemingly illogical connections to phosphate, the railroad and Snook which led to the purchase of our home on Palm Island, where I'm typing these words.

Aware of the phenomenon, I'm now mindful and seek the connections all around us. And, for me, the deepest connections are usually the old ones. I suppose that's why I'm considered "Old School."

Last year, Kim and I were dining in our one restaurant on Palm Island, called Rum Bay Restaurant. If you're not a resident of the island, this restaurant is not the easiest place to get to. You have to get on to the island by the pricey ferry or you come by boat and walk to the restaurant.

We were at our table, waiting for dinner to be served when a lady and man were being escorted to their table by the hostess. As the couple neared our table, I stared at the woman – the kind of stare when you think you recognize someone. At the last minute, my memory clicked and I said (rather loudly) to Kim, "That's Becky Redd." The lady stopped in her tracks, and turned to me as if I was a stalker.

With her husband quickly advancing toward me - the stranger - I scrambled to say, "Becky, I'm Lance Edwards. Do you remember me?"

"Lanceeee..., " she screamed as she gave me a big hug. Now, here's the point...

I knew Becky from the same elementary school where I met Kim. And I haven't seen Becky for over forty years, back when my Mom carpooled us as teenagers to ballroom dance lessons with Mrs. Baker's cotillion. Now, what are the odds that I would run into her in a remote restaurant on an island on that exact date and time? And that she would pass within five feet of our table? It must be millions to one. Yet, it happened.

It turns out that thru her own sequence of events, Becky (who is now Rebecca Hagelin, noted Washington Times columnist) and husband, Andrew Hagelin, live just South of us on Little Gasparilla Island.

Calling In the Cavalry

When Eri died in Houston, it was the Lakeland people in my life who called. Outside of Mom, the first people to call me were brother Brian and best friend, Paul Templin. "What do you need me to do?" was their common question.

More elementary school connections – with no communication in decades - reached out to me as well. Ansley Penkert Masters and Janet Feagle Alter, similar lifetime friends, each called and reached out to me upon hearing the news. School friends, Patty Arnold and Annette Johnston Armstrong, also comprised the regiment.

Jeff Lee, my college roommate who lived in Dallas, showed up and surprised me in Houston at Eri's memorial. "Get to my house in Dallas the minute you can," was his simple instruction. And I did within two weeks; he and his lovely wife, Myra (who I had never met before) took me in and helped me begin the healing process.

With Eri's untimely death, I felt under siege and these connections and outreach to me, in addition to Mom and my family's arrival in Houston, were like the cavalry arriving on the scene. I finally felt hope.

From Old Florida a New Tradition

Now, I'm not a big social media proponent, but thanks to Facebook, these connections have continued – all from relationships decades old, assumed stale but not. All it takes is a spark to restart. Annette Johnston is the sister I never had; the one who busts my chops and vice versa – even after no contact for thirty five years. Diane Moore, is another childhood connection which Kim and I have rekindled in recent history.

It all really comes down to that in life – the people, the times and the connections.

Lance, Kim, Diane Moore Muldoon & Husband Tim Muldoon, Chris Sikes, and Son Jamie Sikes. 2016

It's why Kim and I have established a new annual tradition – Lance and Kim's Fishing Tournament and Anniversary Party, held each year on Palm Island. It started in 2016 with Lance and Kim's Fishing Tournament and Wedding, where we decided to make the wedding a fun event with family and old friends. It was so fun and meaningful to us that we've institutionalized the weekend event as an annual reunion - all bent on the objective of bringing together family and those who Dad called in his poem, "friends of the rarest kind," to rekindle and enjoy the old connections . *As It Should Be.*

Celebrating the Connections - New Annual Tradition

The Back Story

For additional background information, audio and video interviews and/or the unpublished photos for this chapter, visit:

BONUS: The Back Story – Lakeland
http://www.AISBbook.com/Ch05

Chapter 6

Guns and Birds

Now, if the last chapter's topic of Confederate symbols bothered you then put on your seat belt because you're probably not going to like this one. It's about guns. That's right... guns.

Here in Old Florida, we love our guns. Stop. Correction. That's not true. I have no feelings about my guns. To say I love my guns is as silly as extolling my love for my hammer. Or my fishing pole. They're simply inanimate tools that make life easier and separate us from the animals.

What I do covet is my right to own my own guns, made possible by some of my ancestors, and probably some of yours too. Guns do represent to those of Old Florida a way of life – one that was established with the first settlers setting foot in New England and settled with the American Revolution. So we have no feelings about guns. That is, until you try to take them away - just like our Confederate symbols. Then we have strong feelings. You're messing with our way of life, our traditions and our heritage.

Rites of Passage

I grew up around guns. Both Grandpa Edwards and Papa Porter enjoyed hunting so I was exposed at the earliest age to shotguns and rifles. Dad loved to attend a good dove shoot. My step-grandfather, Bob Safford, loved to hunt quail.

Of all my male role models, Grandpa was the most prolific hunter. Beautiful gun racks prominently displayed his Browning shotguns and Remington hunting rifles in his home. Inside could be found the right tool for the task: medium gauge shotguns for Fall dove shoots, larger gauges for Winter turkey stands; rifles for Florida deer hunts. And even bigger caliber rifles for his guided hunts in the Canadian Yukon for big-game rams, moose and bear – whose trophies were proudly showcased in his office. These were the early symbols of manhood to me. When we'd visit his home, I'd sit in front of that gun rack, imagining the day when I would be big enough to handle such weaponry. Guns represented rites of passage to manhood; an earned responsibility.

Responsibility was earned by progression. My first lesson was the Fall dove shoots. Dad called it dove hunting but frankly there was no hunting to it. A dozen men would shoot afternoon doves flying over an open field. There was certainly shooting-skill required in leading a dove or to accomplish a double or triple but other than that, you sat under a tree listening to the Gator game on a transistor radio, waiting for doves to fly by.

The entry level job for a six-year-old boy at a dove shoot was to be a human bird dog. That's right, fetch the downed doves. It required skill too. First, you had to be alert to point out the doves vectoring in within range and then, when shot, to visually mark where they dropped. You see, you couldn't necessarily run into the open field immediately when they dropped for fear of spooking the next flock of low fliers coming within the range of Dad's shotgun. So you had to pay attention and have a good memory.

When Dad gave me the go-ahead, "Go get'em Son," I'd run out into the field, or in some cases thru the barbed wire (pronounced bob-wire) fence and gather the dead birds into the gathering sack sewn into the back of my camouflage suit. When I found one still alive, it was my job to put him out of his misery. At age six that was done with my bare hands. When I earned my first gun, a low-powered BB gun, it was done with a single BB – which signified my first hunting use with a gun.

It was in those dove fields – at age six - where Dad and Grandpa taught me gun safety and responsibility:

"Always treat a gun as if it's loaded."

"Carry it with the barrel facing up or facing down, never cradled in your arm."

"Don't shoot at a low flying dove."

That last lesson was brought home at a dove shoot one afternoon when a young shooter peppered Dad's position with bird shot as the teenager went after a low-flying dove in Dad's vicinity. I suppose I inherited Dad's temper because Dad laid into that poor kid. And rightfully so. A heavier gauge of gun could have seriously injured him or killed him. Although I wasn't there, I learned the lesson too.

After a couple of years of retrieving, I had not yet graduated to a gun but brother Brian was now joining the kennel of human bird dogs. I was already retrieving for Dad so Dad assigned Brian to be Grandpa's retriever. Now, Dad was a fair shot but Grandpa was an excellent shot. Whereas Dad would rejoice if he hit one double (shooting down two birds on one pass) in an afternoon, Grandpa was going after triples. Doubles to him were like home runs to Babe Ruth. After Brian's first dove shoot with Grandpa, he asked Dad, "Do I have to retrieve for Grandpa anymore? He shoots too many." It was hard work retrieving for Grandpa. On the other hand, Dad was an enjoyable afternoon – enjoying nature and picking up an occasional bird in between Florida Gator football scores.

I could always know when dove season opened because it was always around my October 2nd birthday, always opening the first Saturday of that month. As a matter of fact, you can see the young hunter in his new birthday-gift camouflage suit, heading to his first dove shoot, ready for action...

First Dove Shoot, October 1967 – Lance and Dad

It Starts With a BB Gun

After a couple of years as human retriever and gun safety training, I was gifted with my first gun - a BB gun. I received it for Christmas following my ninth birthday. A pellet gun is the entry level gun for a boy to practice gun safety. Mine was a classic Daisy BB gun, made to look like an old 1894 Winchester with cock action and all. It was low-powered so its potency was somewhat limited but nevertheless it could take down a bird at close range or your brother's eye if you were foolish with it. So an additional set of gun safety rules were handed down:

"Don't shoot at any birds or squirrels unless we're hunting."

"Don't shoot up in the air. You don't know where the BB might come down."

Now this last rule was really preparatory for bigger guns. Like I said, the power and range of this BB gun was quite limited but Dad and Grandpa were laying the gun safety foundation for heavier hardware. Mostly, I shot at paper targets or sticks on fence posts, and wounded doves brought down by Dad.

And guess what, I still have that original BB gun. After fifty years, I've kept it. It still shoots and occasionally I load some BB's in it and take target practice in the back yard. It's nostalgic. And symbolic of my first rite of passage to manhood. Some symbols are just that important.

Daisy Model 1894 BB Gun – My First Gun

Becoming Lethal

After a few years of demonstrating that I wouldn't shoot anyone (namely Brian) with my fake Winchester, I graduated into the major leagues: a shot gun. Now, we're talking about real fire power and real responsibility since a shot gun can kill more than a dove, it'll take down a man. I was eleven when I received mine as my big Christmas gift – a single-shot twenty-gauge shot gun. I'd graduated to becoming lethal.

With that new rite, I was also dismissed from the kennel of human bird dogs and Brian was left there solo for a couple of more years as he went thru his orientation. (He would surpass my gun training years later when the Marine Corps entrusted him with automatic machine guns. That reminds me of the story Brian told me about when they were coming back from the glorious victory in Operation Desert Storm. The Marines were chartering commercial airlines to return the conquering warriors home. Their flight had made a layover at an airport and the American flight crew was being changed out. As the Marines were re-boarding, a stewardess detained one of the young Marines over his small pocket knife. With the boarding stalled and the line growing, the gunnery sergeant interceded with the young stewardess, "What's the hold-up here mam?" The young stewardess replied, "I can't let this passenger on board with a lethal weapon." The gunny, defending his combat-proven Marine, replied, "Mam, this *man* is a lethal weapon." He boarded. Semper Fi.)

But an eleven-year-old graduated human retriever doesn't get assigned his own human retriever. You play both sides of the ball. You shoot'em. You collect'em. Not that that was a lot of work for me. I didn't drop too many doves with my single-shot shot gun. Whereas Dad and Grandpa had semi-automatic shotguns that could hold three shells and give them three shots for every dove pass, I only got one shot. If you don't knock'em down the first shot, you're out of luck until the next pass.

The hardest part to hitting a flying bird is learning to lead them. Shooting a flying bird is not the same as shooting a can off of a fence post. That bird's moving and you have to account for the fact that it takes time for the pellet shots of your gun to travel the distance to intersect with that moving object. Which means you don't aim *at* the bird, you aim *in front of* the bird. He needs to fly into your shot pattern. While touring the USS Missouri battleship at Pearl Harbor with Kim, I was reminded the same is true in ground-to-air combat. Painted on the metal heavy-duty anti-aircraft guns were these instructions for the gunners, "*Lead. Dammit. Lead.*" That's what I eventually learned.

Scouts and summer camps filled out my gun safety training and orientation over the next few years. I learned to load and shoot a 22 caliber rifle in the prone and sitting positions. On my way to Eagle Scout, I earned my merit badge in riflery, learning to hold my breath as I gently squeezed the trigger on the rifle and centered my shots on the small black circle at the end of the range. Always always, always, each visit to a new gun range started with gun safety training and basics. It was drilled into us boys. Even an infraction like inadvertently pointing an empty gun at a boy would cost you your range privileges. They were serious – and rightfully so.

Instilling the Values Early

Besides gun training, Scouting taught me many, many life skills. All which have served me in business and my personal life. It is a fabulous organization and one in which its values are reflected in this book thru its instrument, me.

During the writing of this book, President George H.W. Bush (#41) passed away after a complete and full life of service to this country. Like the rest of the nation, I was stirred to emotions by the regality of the funeral and the tributes to this great man, such as the twenty-one cannon salutes over the Potomac and the twenty-one plane flyover at College Station where he was laid to rest. But the image that particularly resonated with me was one of a young cub scout, standing alone, and without any prompting saluting the President's train. Wow. Eight years old and he gets it. That's the Americanism I'm talking about. That's the Old Florida values we stand for and defend. And from that single image on national media, I validated that scouting was still an institution that instills those values.

In 1976, I stood for my Eagle Scout pinning in Lakeland. I was fourteen and Eagle was a goal that I had set for myself as a Cub Scout at age eight. I had gone thru the entire scouting progression: Cub Scouts, then Webelos, and finally Boy Scouts. Mom had seen me get started properly, serving as the den mother for our young Cub Scout den made up of boys in my neighborhood.

Now, six years later, my entire family, along with other scout families and guests, were in attendance at the awards ceremony for various members of my Boy Scout troop. It was a packed house; I was the first Eagle Scout for that troop. I was called up to stand in front of the audience. As I came up, my Scoutmaster asked for any other Eagle Scouts in the audience to join me. Grandpa was the sole man that stood and came to the front. I was very proud to have achieved this honor but to be recognized for it alongside of him – the man I most admired and modeled - was my major rite of passage as a young man.

Lance and Grandpa Edwards, Eagle Scout Ceremony, 1976

It was significant to Grandpa too. He had encouraged me all along the way. In fact, after forty years, he still possessed his Eagle Scout medal. And after the ceremony, he gave his Eagle medal to me, and Mom had it mounted alongside of my mine. Today, they hang proudly in my study. *As It Should Be.*

Two Generations of Eagle Scout Medals

On To Bigger Things – Buck Fever

Dove shoots were an important part of my training and orientation to guns but like I said, I didn't see the sport in sitting under a tree and shooting birds like a carnival duck shoot. I wanted the hunt, the pursuit. By the time I was thirteen, I had graduated to full shotguns and rifles. I could be trusted with any type of gun. And, unbeknownst to me, I was being moved up to bigger game – to play at the varsity level.

Grandpa was hosting one of his big cook-out parties at his Double Diamond Ranch. He was quite the barbecue connoisseur. There were people there from all walks of life. From low station to high, they had come. While finishing up my third plate of his barbecued ribs, Grandpa announced a deer hunt and told his ranch super to get the dogs. He surprised me when he asked, "Lance, you ready to go son?" Having never been on a hunt before, I asked, "Go where?" He quipped, "Deer hunting boy. You grab my 12-gauge and load up." And so I did.

Now our version of deer hunting is not much different than our version of dove hunting; meaning it's a passive sport. The dogs do all the work. In this case, not five-year-old boys but rather real dogs. The hunters are positioned at stations throughout a stand of pines and palmettos – just like shooters around a dove field. Once positioned, the dogs are released at the edge of the scrub to sniff out the scent of a deer. The idea is to scare-up and run a deer past a hunter just like a dove flying past a shooter on a dove field; hence, the passive nature. Anyway, that's the strategy – unknown to me at this moment, being it was my first hunt.

I was in the bed of Grandpa's ranch pickup with a number of men who were being individually dropped off at their respective stands. I was the last one let off and Grandpa said to me, "Now Lance, this is your spot. Keep your eyes open. If a buck comes by, shoot him." "Yes sir," was my reply.

As the truck bounced away over the uneven ground, I could hear the dogs barking in the distance as they were on the run. I was situated on a low berm for a creek that had been cut thru the scrub to convey water throughout the ranch. I figured that if a buck was coming my way, he'd have to jump this berm and creek. As I slipped off the gun safety, I imagined taking my shot at a deer in mid-air leap over the creek. I was ready. At least I thought I was. What did I know.

Then it happened…

I don't know who was more surprised. Me or him.

He had come running up to my stand and then abruptly stopped as he saw me sitting there. He was only ten yards away so I could definitely tell he was a buck (you could only shoot the males). He had a glorious rack. We would call him an eight-point or ten-point, designating how many "tips" he had to his antlers – a real trophy! Excitement surged thru my thirteen-year-old veins. I hopped up, pointed my shotgun and blam, blam, blam, I emptied the 12-gauge shotgun of all three of its buckshot-laden shells. The sound of the blasts echoed off the pine trees as the smoke of the barrel morphed into the wisp of the forest. As I looked down the barrel over the gun sight at the end, I expected to see the fallen buck. Instead, I saw a standing buck - stunned that I had completely shot right over him all three times. He stood standing for many seconds, as if he realized the incredible good fortune that had befallen him that day, to be saved by an obvious case of buck fever (the excitement of a new hunter seeing his first deer and flat out missing his aim). The old fella slowly turned and walked away, as if he was thinking, "Wait til I tell the fellas what happened to me today."

Hearing the blasts, Grandpa's pickup quickly arrived on the scene with him and his ranch super in the cab. "What happened?" he asked. Embarrassed, I had to explain how I missed my first buck. I explained how close the target had stood to me. As I was speaking to Grandpa, the super got out of the driver's seat and started poking around where I said the buck had stood. I could see him checking the ground. When he came back, he said to Grandpa, "Tillis, I don't see any blood to trail." Then he leaned over and tried to whisper so I couldn't hear him, "Tillis, I'm not even sure there was a deer here. I think the boy imagined it."

It was rare when I ever saw my grandfather go after a man but he did that day. He railed, "Goddammit! If Lance said he saw a buck, there was a buck here. Shut your goddamn mouth." Case closed. The super retreated into his side of what had just become a very small truck cab. As bad as I felt about letting my grandfather down, I was proud of how he stood up for me at that deer stand that day. I've never forgotten it.

Helluva Shot

Unfortunately, I was never presented the chance to redeem myself over that bout of buck fever. Although I was invited back to other deer hunts, I never again saw a deer over my gun sights. I was "skunked" as they say. Whether sitting in a tree stand alone in the scrub or being positioned on the "dog run," I've never had another deer come within my range. That's okay. I'm not a big fan; it's not like me and Snook. I just welcomed the chance to redeem myself with my grandfather.

However, I did see a buck come into Brian's gun range one freezing December morning at the ranch. It was Christmas break from college and Grandpa had organized a hunt on a Saturday between Christmas and New Year's – an excuse for the men to get out of the house and away from long-winded relatives. My college roommate, Jeff Lee, had come to town during the break and we'd been hitting the night life hard. Getting up before daylight was not high on our priorities that Saturday morning but the Kid (our nickname for Jeff) had graciously agreed to join Brian and me for the hunt that morning (I didn't dare turn down an invitation from Grandpa).

In the pre-dawn darkness, we drove the forty minutes to the ranch where we met the group and took our assigned positions. In this instance, the three of us were to be along a barbed wire fence looking over a field of palmettos, against a backdrop of a beautiful pine island - a sight frankly wasted on us since we were tired (on a scant four hours sleep) and freezing. But we sucked it up, secretly imagining how great it would be to be back in the rack.

In the cold, the dogs started their chase with the barking coming nearer. It's never ceased to amaze me how hard a dog will track and chase a deer. They're like the postman. Neither cold, nor dark nor slashing palmetto fronds deter these dogs on the scent. In any event, it seemed like the action was moving in our direction.

I don't know who saw him first but the shout came out, "There he is. Get'em Brian!"

Brian was armed not with a shotgun like the Kid and me but rather a Remington rifle with a scope. And there were two tactical problems for Brian. The buck was at least one hundred yards away (out of shotgun range) and running – a nearly impossible shot for a rifle. At least with a shotgun, you have a pattern spread to hit your target – if he's within range. We could just see the deer leaping over the palmettos, his distinctive white tail up in the air with each leap. Even from one hundred yards, we could tell he was a beauty with a full rack – trophy quality. The good news was that he was running straight across Brian's shooting area with a full side view.

Brian was sixteen at the time, fully indoctrinated by then in the use of shotguns and rifles. He coolly leveled the rifle on a fence post and let off the first shot. The deer kept running. He reloaded and let off the second shot. Brian not only had to lead the deer like a dove but he had to account for the deer's vertical up and down movements. The deer was increasing his distance from Brian and I figured this one's gonna get away too because it's just too hard of a shot. But, despite that, the Kid and I simultaneously yelled out, "Get'em Brian." Brian lets off a third shot and the deer drops amidst the palmettos like a sack of potatoes.

Shouts emanated from that fence line as we all hopped the barbed wire and ran the hundred yards to where the deer lay. The older men, the seasoned hunters, also gathered up around the deer with us – a ritual going back I suppose to cave men who've taken down a wooly mammoth or such. Brian accepted congratulations from all around and slaps on the back for his first deer. No buck fever here. It was a helluva shot. An impossible shot. The best shot I've ever seen. And that was before the Marines even got ahold of him. *As It Should Be.*

It's Hard to Be Cool

When I was home from college on Christmas break, Grandpa would often hand me the keys to the ranch and say, "Son, you're free to go over and sit for a turkey." Turkey was yet another bird we hunted, although I never developed a knack for it. It was another passive form of hunting where, on the cold and usually wet ground, you sat in the dark of the pre-dawn hours waiting for a hapless gobbler to meander by.

Grandpa excelled at it. He actually had a special shotgun just for turkey shooting – a 10-gauge. That's the largest bore shotgun made, designed for bringing down geese and turkey. He would always tell me how he caught three turkey running down a cow trail, in a single column, one morning and bagged all three with a single shot.

I did it mostly because I enjoyed the challenge and the opportunity to get out into the Florida scrub. But I wasn't very good at it. I never developed the skill, mostly the patience, for turkey hunting.

One December morning in 1979, home from college, I woke at 5AM, loaded up my shotgun and drove my little '68 Mercury Cougar out to the Double Diamond near Polk City, Northeast of Lakeland. It was still dark (and cold) when I got there. I finally was able to open the daisy chain of Master locks at the main gate and entered the ranch.

The old Cougar managed to navigate the ranch road okay. It was a new moon and so my headlights were the only illumination shooting across the cow pastures and on to the pine islands and scrub. I parked the car near the edge of an island and walked a couple hundred yards or so to a gap between two pine islands, like a pass connecting two bodies of water. I found a spot just inside the scrub and took my stand – in the mud.

This is where the patience part of turkey hunting becomes important. Because now the name of the game is wait. Wait for sunrise. Wait (and hope) a rafter of turkeys come by. I'd been taught to be perfectly still because turkey are skittish birds and the slightest movement can send them scampering out of range.

When you're sitting in the cold damp mud in the dark, you think about a lot of things. Namely, "What am I doing here?" And "I wonder if a turkey is going to come by." To further test your commando stillness skills, you have the occasional mosquito (even in cold weather) to buzz around your mosquito hood.

With sunrise, you're able to start taking an assessment of your position and the wait becomes a little less tedious because at least now you have things to look at. Is that a turkey? Is that a deer? After all, there's no telling what might come walking by on their morning walk. Basically, you get to witness the Florida scrub waking up in the morning. It's a beautiful thing.

That morning, I had been hunkered down in that damp, cold mud for about an hour past sunrise when I heard it. It was definitely movement. Something coming thru the pass from my right, out of view, but moving steadily. I assumed the best frozen-man position I could muster (not hard as I was actually freezing). Not a muscle moved for fear of spooking the game. Whatever it was, it was definitely coming my way. I gently and quietly flipped the safety on the shotgun.

Then I saw it…

It was a small bunch of cows taking their morning stroll, doing what those dumb animals do best, blindly following the cow in front of them. One cow had moved that morning so the whole gang had to trail along. "That's okay," I thought. "They'll clear out soon enough."

And that's when it happened. The event that forever changed my turkey hunting future…

Remember, I was carefully concealed amidst the bushes and scrub, squatting in the damp mud, with my full garb camouflage suit and hat, including mosquito net around my head. I was invisible. The closest cow was maybe fifteen yards away from me.

She stopped, turned and looked right at me. And mooed!

That dumb cow had walked up, looked at me and basically shot me the finger. She was laughing at me. It took every ounce of self-restraint not to bag a cow that morning, but I knew it'd be a little difficult explaining to Grandpa why there was a cow draped over the hood of the Cougar.

It was at that point, I stood up, walked back to the car and never squatted for a turkey stand again. It's hard to be cool as a turkey hunter when even the cows are calling you out.

Rafter of Wild Turkey (at Paul Templin's Country Home)

The Robalo Club With Guns

In Chapter 1, I introduced the Robalo Club – that group of irreverent Lakeland men who shared such an affinity for Snook, they created a Hilton in the Everglades wilderness, otherwise known as the Cabin. Well, that same affinity for Snook fishing carried over to duck hunting as well - but watered down, unlike their whisky.

Each year, duck season in Florida opens up the weekend before Thanksgiving and, just like the migratory water fowl they sought, the Robalo Club members flocked to Lake Kissimmee. Joined by other friends who enjoyed the comradery, the event was known as Duck Camp – an annual tradition. Sure there were some real duck fanatics like my Uncle David Edwards who to this day is known as "Spoon" because of his enthusiasm for Spoonbills but, for most of the other attendees, including Dad, Duck Camp was a reason to get away and gather with those "friends of the rarest kind." That is, it was really just a Thanksgiving version of the Everglades.

Whereas I was invited to the Cabin when I was seven, I wasn't invited to Duck Camp until I was seventeen.

Totally in character with the times and the members, the Duck Camp excursion started at a bar – a Lakeland lounge named El Greco. It was there that the members and friends rendezvoused to caravan the Duck Camp parade over to Kissimmee. Believe it or not, some of us actually had our gear and shotguns stacked around the lounge awaiting our assigned rides. I know it's probably difficult to imagine shotguns stacked in a bar with a bunch of duck hunters but that was the scene in 1978.

I was assigned to Dad's friend, Leroy. Leroy was not a Robalo Club member but he was a great guy. He fit the mold: a self-made man who loved to hang out with his like-minded friends. He was hilarious in that group.

I loaded my gun and gear in the back of Leroy's pickup and he declared me the designated driver (back before the term was even coined). Before we pulled out of the parking lot, he said, "Lance, go back there and pour me a new drink. You'll find whisky in the igloo (cooler)." At seventeen, I had never mixed a drink before but I figured I had to learn some time and now was as good a time as any. I hopped out of the cab and packed a styrofoam cup with ice and half-filled it with whisky. Not knowing what to do next, I asked, "Leroy, do you want something in it?" (Me thinking water or soda.) "Yea, ice," was his reply. Ice it is.

Duck Camp was a dozen or so men gathered around the campfire at night doing what men do best at a campfire – telling lies and opining their views on world domination. The story-telling over drinks was the best part of Duck Camp, the part that frankly most of them were there for. In between, there was shooting at ducks from a duck blind in the early mornings. But unlike dove shooting, with duck shooting you have to actually be smarter than the bird. There's strategy in where and how you deploy your decoys to lure the high-flying ducks down to within range of your gun. But mostly you're there for the comradery.

With this group of men, there were side bets and pools on everything from most birds killed today, most birds killed on the trip, first on the water, last back, ugliest sister. You name it. It was a hoot to observe. Even better if you could indulge.

There's a legend about Duck Camp – which occurred before my time. There's a large popular island in the middle of Lake Kissimmee where the hunters loved to set up their blinds and decoys. It was (maybe still is) owned by the Lykes Brothers Corporation. Rumor had it that the Lykes Brothers kept a lion on this island. That's right. An African island. Why? Beats me but just go along with me on this. It was pretty much an accepted fact by everyone except Spoon (my Uncle David). After all, that island was Spoon's favorite spot for bringing down the big ones. And he wasn't giving it up for any silly rumor of a lion.

It all changed one pre-dawn morning when Spoon, all alone in his blind on the Lykes Brothers island, heard a roar from the island's scrub. If you've ever seen a duck take off from the water with his feet scampering across the waves, that was the scene of David high-tailing it across the water to his boat from his land-bound blind. I've never asked David if the story's true but if it's not, it's *As It Should Be*.

Uncle David "Spoon" Edwards Passing the Tradition On
To Grandsons Xander and Nick Pivovarnik, 2017

Finally, The True Hunt

Up until now, we've covered all types of "ambush-hunting." That is, you sit and wait for the game to come to you. And then you shoot it. It's an ambush; *passive* hunting. Yes, there's the selection of the best spot and the proper cover and even the decoys but for me the real hunt is when you *actively* track down your prey. Now, there's sport and thinking in that. And that's why my favorite hunt was quail hunting.

Nana's second husband, my step-grandfather (Robert Safford who I knew as Uncle Bob) was the one who introduced me to it. Quail hunting has it all: the planning, the pursuit, the burst of excitement, and quality time in the unspoiled Florida scrub.

Uncle Bob had two bird dogs (pointers) who he had trained to trail quail. Each Christmas break from college, he'd graciously ask me if I wanted to go quail hunting and I'd enthusiastically answer yes. We'd hunt Grandpa's ranch at Double Diamond. (Even though Uncle Bob was married to Grandpa's ex-wife, they still had a great relationship.)

Uncle Bob would stagger the dogs on their runs. He'd let one dog out to find the scent of the ground-bound quail. Just like the deer dogs who tracked deer, his bird dogs loved the opportunity to get out into that Florida scrub as much as I did. Just as I came to know the Everglades' mangrove life from a front-row seat navigating the narrow creeks with Dad, I came to experience the Florida scrub by walking it with my Uncle Bob. Miles and miles of it. The act of experiencing Florida, unspoiled and untouched - exactly as my Cracker ancestors found it, connected me to the Old Florida I loved.

We'd trail the dog in the knee-high grass waiting for the sign – the "point." Quail get around – less by flying – and more by walking and running along the ground. In fact, they nest on the ground. The dog would track the scent of their walking. When the covey was in sight of the dog – and he was practically standing over them, the dog would stop, extend his nose straight out, bend his front leg and stick his tail straight back to point us to the quail. A point is a beautiful sight to behold – a tradition that's been carried on for hundreds of years.

A Pointer On the Point

Uncle Bob and I would release our safeties, being mindful of the location of the other, and we'd slowly approach the dog's point. Once we were in position, Uncle Bob would give the command and the pointer would "flush the covey" meaning the dog would step into the cluster of birds forcing it to take flight immediately in front of us.

There's a distinctive whirring and flapping sound as a dozen quail simultaneously leap into the air. If I was on the left, I would pick and shoot the birds flying to my side, Uncle Bob would take those on the right. It was a harmonious symphony of man and dog working together. Once shot, the pointer would retrieve the dead birds in his mouth and bring them to Uncle Bob.

I wish I had an actual panoramic picture to show you. I can visualize it all in my mind. The golden Fall grass, the brown and green of the pine islands, the black and gold of the quail, the sound of the pines swaying in the breeze. Just like the scene of Dewey George rowing our boat in the Glades along the mangrove line, I need to likewise have this scene captured to canvas from my memory. It is indeed Old Florida as well.

Harvey, Take Your Best Shot

In August 2017, Kim and I were moving into our new home in Florida on Palm Island. As we moved in, on the other side of the Gulf of Mexico, Hurricane Harvey struck the Texas coast.

For the next week, we watched on the television the devastation in Houston as Harvey flooded the city. With my office and house in Houston, I was particularly keen to the happenings. Our house there is upstream of the Addicks Dam and Reservoir, which quickly filled due to the deluge of fifty inches of rainfall concentrated on the city in just three days. As the water accumulated, I tracked the level of the reservoir online and compared it to the elevation of the house. Hoping for hope, I finally had to admit defeat and told Kim, "That's it. The Houston house is flooded." When the waters receded and we were finally able to return to Houston, we found that we had had three inches of water standing in the house for three days.

Fortunately, Kim's cousin, Greg King, owned a water and salvage company in Tennessee, and was on the scene even before we were with his equipment and crew emptying the house and stripping the sheetrock before mold could set in. With Greg as "Mr. Johnny-on-the-Spot," we were in much better shape than most Houstonians. Thanks Greg!

When we arrived, we assessed the damage and the work ahead of us. With his crew, Greg showed me how they had gathered everything up. Down to the finest detail, they had organized everything far better than I would have imagined. But once we were away from his crew, Greg quietly pulled me to the side and said, "I found something that I wasn't sure what to do with." He led me into the garage and there, tucked away in the corner, were my guns. One was an old pump shotgun given to me by Dad and my two other guns which belonged to Grandpa, and I inherited when he died.

I had completely forgotten about them; I haven't hunted in decades. Now, due to Harvey, they were in really bad shape. Under our bed and underwater for three days, they had been exposed to the nastiest of nasty water, and were covered in rust. Their inner workings were already jamming.

Once I got the house demo underway, my first priority was to tend to those guns. It wasn't the monetary value. I could replace those guns for far less than the cost of restoration. It was the symbolic value. They are symbols of my rite of passage to manhood; a right I had earned starting at age six as that human retriever. They were reminders of the dove shoots with Dad, the deer hunt when Grandpa dressed down his ranch super and the walks in the Florida scrub with Uncle Bob.

I found the best gunsmith in Houston and dropped the guns off; as did hundreds of other gun owners who experienced the same fate as me and held the same affinity for their guns. I didn't even ask what the cost was going to be. It didn't matter. They are priceless to me.

It was over a year before I got the call that the guns were finally ready. I'm happy to report that they're better than ever and tucked away safely – this time in a place that's far more high and dry. *As It Should Be.*

The Back Story

For additional background information, audio and video interviews and/or the unpublished photos for this chapter, visit:

BONUS: The Back Story – Guns and Birds
http://www.AISBbook.com/Ch06

Chapter 7

All I Really Need to Know I Learned in _____

On September 24, 1985, I was on the eve of my 24th birthday and had just successfully defended my Master's thesis. Except for the signing of the diploma, my formal education was officially complete with a Master's degree in Chemical Engineering from the University of Notre Dame. It couldn't have come sooner. I was tired of schooling, tired of the bitter cold Indiana winter and missing Florida. With one week til my 24th birthday and five weeks til I started a new job in Houston, I loaded up my old '68 Cougar, hooked up yet another U-Haul trailer, and made a beeline for Lakeland.

By the time I hit Lakeland two days later, it was noon so the first place I targeted was El Greco's, with U-Haul and all. El Greco's was a non-fancy (plain) Greek restaurant and lounge. The bar was the real attraction. Being lunchtime, I knew I'd find Dad and the regulars of the Robalo Club there at the lounge having lunch and cocktails. And I meant to surprise them like the conquering warrior come home.

Sure enough, Dad's car was in the parking lot and as I entered the dark lounge, it was cheers, hugs and pats on the back. Drinks all around. Once the celebration had calmed down and the men began to individually leave to return to their respective businesses, it was Dad and me alone.

"I'm really proud of you Son," he said. "Congratulations." "Thanks Dad," was my reply.

Then he hit me with what has always stuck with me, "Of course, you realize don't you that despite your Notre Dame Master's degree, your real education happened here?"

After all, Dad had taken Brian and me with him into lounges since I was five years old. Over those dozen years of my "real education" before departing for college, I'd always sit next to Dad, surrounded by his like-minded friends, and hear them discuss their challenges and their victories. And, today, with fifty years of hindsight, I can see that Dad was right. My real education was there.

If you've ever seen an episode of Mad Men where they drank and smoked over lunch, that was the scene in the 1960's and 1970's of my private classroom. Topics covered everything under the sun: golf, football, women, gambling, business, chess, fishing, hunting, the OJ futures market. You name it and I can share wisdom from this front row seat of my real education. I could fill a tome on those learnings.

Years ago there was a popular book, *All I Really Need to Know I Learned in Kindergarten*. Well, this chapter might be titled, "All I Really Need to Know I Learned in _Bars_."

Of course, I say that somewhat tongue in cheek but the experiences of being around those Old Florida men, as a boy, whether in bars, boats, fish camps, or duck camps left a lasting impression on who I became and how I carried myself - whether in Lakeland, Houston, Paris or Tokyo. Within this short chapter, I'd like to give you a glimpse into what I mean.

Lance and Dad at El Greco's 1984

Jackkkkk!!!

If you've ever seen the TV show, Cheers, you'll remember that there was a regular there, named Norm, who every time he walked in the door, the patrons yelled "Normmmm!!!" Every bar worth entering has a regular like Norm. The Cheers writers got that right. However, there's one detail they got wrong. Bar regulars are always named Jack, not Norm. I suspect the producers changed the name to protect the innocent.

We had a Jack at El Greco's. We have a Jack at our one bar on Palm Island. It's as if it's a regulation put out by the Alcohol and Beverage Commission that each bar must maintain one Jack on premises to sustain their liquor license. Whatever the reason, "Jacks" are always entertaining, affable men who can get along with anyone. Regular fixtures that make the place worth hanging out - knowledgeable on practically all topics across the vast spectrum of human experience. Incredibly patient. Tolerant. Frankly, they just don't care. They've advanced beyond sweating the details. They take life one day at a time.

Want to know a quick, sure fire way to determine if a bar has character and worth visiting? Simple. Call the bar and ask for Jack. If they reply, "Who's Jack," it's guaranteed to be boring. Pass. On the other hand, if they answer, "Hang on," you've got a winner.

Now, if you get a reply, "Which one," drag all your buddies down there. And hold on. It's gonna be an experience. (Just sayin'.)

Size Matters

Now let's define bar. I don't mean loud night clubs or giant honky-tonks. Bar, in my world, means what I knew as a *lounge* – usually an extension of a restaurant. El Greco's was El Greco's Restaurant and Lounge. And, as the name implies, you went there to "lounge" around with compadres; to relax, laugh, to have a drink. Basically, Starbucks with a liquor license.

Usually dark, a lounge has a formal bar top but it's surrounded by tables. Dark seems to be a key ingredient so you can lose track of time. In fact, there should be no windows for that reason alone. When you walked into El Greco's during the day, you'd better take off your sunglasses beforehand because you were walking into a cave. Dark was also good so that you couldn't see the stains in the carpet or the peeling wall paper. And after your eyes adjusted and you ultimately walked back out again in the middle of the day, the daylight was blinding; it was as if you were walking straight into the sun.

And as far as size, the smaller the better. You don't want giant Urban Cowboy Gilley's-type places but small intimate lounges. El Greco's had eight round tables. Palm Island's bar has five. And, of course, you have your "usual" spot. At El Greco's, Dad's usual spot was close to the wall with the phone jack because… he had a private phone installed.

I kid you not. In the period before Internet and cell phones, people communicated via landlines. And because Dad's occupation as a citrus man mandated that he continually be in contact with growers and buyers, he had a private phone for the two to three hours he'd spend for lunch every day at El Greco's. Of course, anyone could use it but they didn't. It was "Arthur's phone."

In fact, Dad's business tool kit consisted of two items: a yellow legal pad and a phone. On the legal pad, he kept phone numbers, action items and business notes. The pages would be curled back as he progressed thru the pad. He never tore off a page.

He was a Renaissance man because that business model has now become the norm in today's Information Age where I run my business from anywhere using my version of a legal pad (my laptop) and a cell phone.

A funny story on that and I'll move on…

Last Laugh

Recall at the turn of the 21st century in 1999, there was the big "Y2K scare." Computers were prevalent, unlike they were in 1900, and the concern was how would late 20th century computers respond to a date of 2000. Since early programmers used just the last two digits to designate the year in their code (for example: "61" or "81"), what would happen on January 1, 2000 when the two digits for the year would be "00?" After all, no one had considered this possibility with the nascent computer industry in 1980. Would the computers think the year was 1900 or 2000 or 1500? Would banking computers come to a screeching halt? Would our nuclear missile arsenal launch? Would we have Armageddon? That "Y2K scare" was on everyone's mind.

In 1999, I was in the corporate world, working for Aspen Technology, a publicly traded software company that sold and installed computer control software in every major petrochemical plant around the world. Our software (some of it installed and programmed by me) was mission critical to operating these massive plants where high pressures and temperatures were involved in the conversion of crude oil into the products that drive the world today: gasoline, ethylene, plastics. Big stakes in these plants. And, so there was a real concern about protecting their computer control systems for Y2K.

At that time, I ran North American Sales for the petroleum sector of the company and I can tell you 1999 was a busy time for us (and every software company) because all of the corporate players were buying upgraded software by the truckload that was "Certified Y2K Compliant;" meaning that it was immune to 1900 versus 2000 year distinctions. No manager or board was going to allow January 1, 2000 to hit without ensuring its software was Y2K Compliant. It was a banner revenue year for me. But December 31, 1999 was an anxious day – for two reasons. One, it was the eve of a New Century and two, would we survive it? Of course, we're here so that tells you what happened. Big nothing. Anyway, back to Dad the Renaissance Man...

Unbeknownst to anyone, January 1, 2000 would be Dad's last New Year. He died Christmas Day, 2000. Brian, Nana and I were there. In the following week, when Brian and I were going thru Dad's things, I found his yellow legal pad. As typical, it was heavily used and the yellow-lined pages were curled back around the spine and Dad's distinctive handwriting was cast across the pages. But when I un-curled all the pages back into their original form, I could see on the top page, Dad had written in big letters across that cover page, *"This Legal Pad is Certified Y2K Compliant."*

As usual, Dad got the last laugh.

Defying the Rules

Lunch at El Greco's was when all of the regulars of the Robalo Club would gather, at least the regulars I came to know and who served as the contrarian set of role models to what I was being taught in school. In school, I was taught from Day One of Grade One that the model to success was this: *"Study hard, work hard and get good grades. Then go to a good college where you'll study hard, work hard and get good grades. All so you can get a good job."* In fact, if I would have asked any one of Dad's friends at the El Greco lunch table the secret to success, I'm confident each one – to a man – would have given me the same advice.

It was what school preached, it's what my parents preached, and it's what Nana basically said when she threw me out of consideration in entering the family citrus business. She even tried it on Dad as a teenager when she told him that he had to attend college, and his first two years had to be outside of the state of Florida. She did concede he could ultimately return to his friends at the University of Florida but not until he had completed two years of study out of state. And Nana had further decided that Atlanta would be the proper place for young Arthur Edwards to spend his two years.

Dad told me this story several times over the years, and each time he recounted it, he would grin and confide that when he heard the edict from Nana, he felt like Brer Rabbit who had just been captured by Brer Fox, slyly pleading in secret, "Do anything to me but please don't throw me into that briar patch."

(If you don't know the story, you've been deprived in your education. Go read "Uncle Remus," written in 1881.)

Dad spent two fun-filled years at Emory University in Atlanta. All he really learned was that college was not for him. So at age nineteen, he quit school, married Mom and joined the family citrus business as the third and final Edwards generation to enter citrus.

So everyone around me, including the lunch regulars at El Greco's, were giving me the same advice. Yet, I noticed that none of them had heeded that advice. Those men around the cocktail tables at lunch in El Greco were certified unemployable, meaning they were far too independent to take orders from anyone else. I don't know which, if any, had a college degree but from what I could tell none received any value from it other than perhaps their fraternity connections.

Like modern-day Florida Crackers, they were each self-made and self-employed. They had a common set of rules, it was just a different rule set from what I was being taught in my formal education. But at the core of their rules was this: *show respect for men, the traditions and the land*; it was the basis for "The Code" – an unwritten set of rules on successful living, handed down from our Revolutionary War ancestors down thru our Florida Cracker great-grandfathers. If you just followed those core rules, you'd be fine. Outside of that, you were free to write your own rules. Life was as you made it.

Some were doing well, some were just getting by but they were each in control of their own schedules and lives. That's why they could afford to come and go as they wished at El Greco's, or anywhere for that matter. They had selected that choice of freedom over the "recommended route." As Henry David Thoreau wrote and as Dad had hanging in his home, they each "marched to the beat of a different drummer."

It would take me twenty five years before I discovered their rules of independence were superior and to gather up the courage to do the same as them - and completely disregard the world's conventional advice. It took me that long to discover we can indeed write our own rules – as long as we follow the core rules: *show respect for men, traditions and the land* – all of which I first learned from them. And that's all I really needed to know.

The Back Story

For additional background information, audio and video interviews and/or the unpublished photos for this chapter, visit:

BONUS: The Back Story – All I Really Need to Know…
http://www.AISBbook.com/Ch07

Chapter 8

This is Gator Country

No book on Florida would be proper without religious traditions. No, not Judeo-Christian traditions but rather college football traditions.

Only Texas can rival Florida for the number of football disciples (fans) and outright talent. There's so much high school football talent in Florida that the state commands the most consistent number of Top 20 college football programs of all states: Florida State University, University of Miami, University of South Florida, University of Central Florida (new addition) and of course, the greatest of them all... the University of Florida Gators.

At this point, I should warn any Florida Gator football rivals, you may take exception to a few of the claims made in this chapter. But know they are the most scientifically-based, unbiased, objective collection and statement of facts ever gathered this side of a congressional re-election speech. (In other words, pick out the parts you like; take the rest with a grain of salt.) And, as always, please save your cards and letters.

America's Sport

College football is indeed America's sport. It has all that Americans love - namely, a good fight. General Patton unmasked this love in his profound (and profane) speech to the Third Army in WWII:

> *"Men, all this stuff you hear about America not wanting to fight, wanting to stay out of the war, is a lot of bullsh*t. Americans love to fight. All real Americans love the sting and clash of battle. When you were kids, you all admired the champion marble shooter, the fastest runner, the big-league ball players and the toughest boxers. Americans love a winner and will not tolerate a loser.*
>
> *Americans play to win all the time. That's why Americans have never lost and will never lose a war. The very thought of losing is hateful to Americans. Battle is the most significant competition in which a man can indulge. It brings out all that is best and removes all that is base."*
>
> - *General George S. Patton, Address to Third Army, 1944*

It is our love of a good fight, a good battle, combined with the traditions and youthful memories of an alma mater which draws college football's fans, unlike any other American sport. Beyond this, you find a strong common love between college football and all things military. It's why we have military fly-overs at the game's opening, the presenting of the colors, the singing of the National Anthem, and the standing ovation for alumnus veterans at half-time. Our love of college football is intertwined with our respect for all things military.

Don't believe me? Well, just look at the language, borrowed from the military, to describe college football's actions: we have an *offense* and a *defense*; we *"defend our turf;"* we make a *"goal-line stand;"* we play on a *"gridiron;"* we have *"fight songs;"* we describe the game's controlled violence as a *"good clean hit;"* and to win the game, we throw the *"long bomb."*

Goal-Line Stand. Gators Stop The LSU Tigers Cold

My Houston friend, Jim Martinez, has graciously invited me in the past to attend Texas A&M football games with him and his sons. What an opportunity. If you want to see the military parallels with college football proudly on display, watch a Texas A&M game. There, the whole of the student body stands for the entire game in symbolic representation of the "Twelfth Man" – the multi-decades tradition symbolizing each student's willingness to step in if a member of the eleven-man team goes down on the field (women included). College football is the American (and civilized) version of Roman gladiators, with the twist of religious-like traditions.

College Football Spirit on Display
Texas A&M Student Body

As far as I'm concerned, there's no comparison between college and professional football. Yes, professional football is Sunday afternoon gladiator sessions but, at least for me, they lack the traditions of college football. For example, there is no marching band in professional football. And it's not really football without the band beating out the traditional fight songs. Now, some of the (other teams') fight songs are grating (like FSU's tomahawk chop and Tennessee's Rocky Top) but nevertheless when played regularly with the controlled violence of the gridiron clash, they illicit emotions from alumnus and fans like nothing else. That middle-aged fan in the stands can feel the fight again, shouting at the top of his lungs, "Hold the line defense. Hold the line." It's the spirit of college football which I've never found in professional ball.

Gators Marching Band Pregame – The Spirit of College Football

That spirit is heightened each season with the annual "homecoming" – the chance for alumni to return home to their alma mater (Latin for "nourishing mother"), confident that the traditions they celebrated decades ago still live strong; that is, a return to all things comfortable. Homecoming boasts a Homecoming Parade, a Homecoming Queen, and a Homecoming Party – all traditions exclusive to college football, and foreign to professional football.

Finally, the players on college football teams play because they want to, not because they are paid to. Yes, of course, some of the college players aspire to receive a huge NFL contract at the end of their college careers but only a minority of players ever go pro.

Most play because they want to represent their school they grew up cheering for or it's what their father did – it's the tradition. Some just want to be able to play that one down to tell their future grandkids of the grand old days.

You don't find these same emotional attractors in any other college or professional sport. Not basketball, not baseball, nowhere else. College football is America's sport.

Florida's Team

Dad used to say that if you put a dozen random boys in a sandlot field in Florida, and threw in a football, fifteen thousand people would show up. Whereas college football is America's sport, Florida is its altar. We revere college football. And at the center of our reverence is the Florida Gators.

As a boy, and up thru high school, I was one of those kids with the football in a sandlot. We'd play no-pad, full-contact football. It's just what you did. We didn't have pads or helmets. And we loved it. You take the most mild mannered, nerdy Florida kid and put him on the defensive line on a pass rush and you'll discover his primeval instincts. This metamorphosis to cave man aggression (albeit controlled) has always fascinated me; it goes back to General Patton's thesis that Americans love a good battle. That's what football was to us – a friendly but serious battle of collisions.

I'm not sure how the Gators became Florida's most popular team other than the fact the University of Florida's football program is by far the oldest. I never attended there; neither did my parents or my grandparents. In fact, most Gator fans never attended the university; we were just raised to cheer the Gators. They represented Florida in America's sport.

FOOTBALL

It was hard being a Gator fan for their first sixty years or so. The Gators never seemed to be able to win the big game. Growing up, the most common saying I recall about the Gators was "Wait til next year." In the 1970's, the Gators were 0 and 53 in the Southeastern Conference Championships – meaning that for 53 consecutive years they had failed to achieve a single conference championship, let alone a national championship.

The Gators always seemed to get upset by a less talented team or fumble the ball at that critical moment when all the marbles counted. It was both exciting and agonizing to be a Florida Gator fan. But there was always next year and the hope that the football gods would then look favorably down upon our beloved Gators. The only redeeming fact, as a Gator fan, was that the other Florida football schools were worse.

Nevertheless, despite their record or our frustrations, we'd religiously listen to Florida Gator football each Saturday. It was tradition. In the Fall, our lives were scheduled around the Gator games. If I was retrieving birds for Dad at a dove shoot on a Saturday and the Gators were playing that afternoon, rest assured Dad would have the Gator game playing on a transistor radio under that tree. As would every other shooter. Around the dove field, you'd simultaneously hear touchdown-inspired shouts of joy, fumble-induced curses and the blasts of shot guns as the Gators battled and the doves flew in.

That scheduling of our lives around the Gator games has continued with me into middle-age. You see, with my business, I conduct monthly real estate seminars around the country. And we publish our annual seminar schedule in advance – all except the Fall months of September, October and November. I can't publish those months until the University of Florida releases the Gators' football schedule for the upcoming year. And once released, I never schedule my seminars over rivalry game weekends. That would be sacrilegious to miss one of those.

When Kim and I decided to get married three years ago (billed as "Lance and Kim's Fishing Tournament and Wedding"), we selected October as the month for the ceremony. My only suggestion to Kim was, "Let's do it during the Gators' bye week, the week before the Georgia rivalry game, when they won't be playing and we won't miss a game." When it turned out that the only Saturday available in October for our wedding venue was the same weekend as the Gators' Homecoming game, I countered with, "Honey, I don't want you to question my love for you but if there aren't at least TV's broadcasting the Gator game at the wedding reception, I won't be there." Yes, we take our Gator football seriously.

Lance and Kim's Fishing Tournament and Wedding

Today, when we schedule our annual "Lance and Kim's Fishing Tournament and Anniversary Party" in October, we pick a weekend of a Gators' away game. If we pick a home game weekend, there's a good chance no one will show up. On the other hand, I've discovered that just like you can attract fifteen thousand Floridians if you throw some kids into a sandlot with a football, you can likewise draw a mob of middle-aged Gator fans from around the state to your home if you offer a Gator away-game on TV and free booze.

Friends and Family Watching the Gator Game on Palm Island.
Lance and Kim's Annual Fishing Tournament & Anniversary, 2018

Florida's Messiah

I mentioned that the Gators were 0-53 in conference championships when I was growing up in the 1960's and 1970's. They weren't very good. Well, that all changed in 1990...

By 1989, despite countless prayers by the fan base, nothing had really changed with the Gators. A string of mediocre coaches had come and gone, continuing the pattern of mediocre play spiked with moments of excited anticipation but dashed by stupid mistakes. Still, the Gators had failed to secure the elusive conference championship. Finally, after decades of mediocre play and countless pleas to the heavens, the Gators had their prayers answered. It's said that God answers all prayers but in his own good time and on his terms. Well, he may have been slow to answer but his response was perfect. In 1990, he sent us our football savior.

In 1990, the university had fired yet another coach following a disappointing season. And they were on the search again. This time, however, the university brought home their favorite Gator, Steve Spurrier, as the new "Head Ball Coach." Spurrier was not just some football coach; he was the Ultimate Gator.

Nearly twenty five years earlier, in 1966, Spurrier had been the Gators' star quarterback and its first (and until then only) Heisman Trophy winner – college football's recognition of the best player. In the vast sea of time of Gator football mediocrity, Steve Spurrier's Heisman symbolized the single greatest moment in Gator football history.

Since his days as a player, and following a decade of uninspired professional play, Spurrier had continually succeeded in a number of coaching positions – moving up in the ranks to the point where he was currently Head Coach at Duke University (coincidentally my alma mater). He had taken a Duke team loaded with egg heads and converted them into something respectful on a football field – a feat not achieved since WWII. So when the Gators needed a decent football coach (yet again) in 1990, up-and-coming Coach Spurrier got the call, "Help's needed. Come home." The Ultimate Gator heeded the call and returned to Gainesville. His arrival changed everything – forever – about Florida Gator football.

It was beautiful. It was as if the Gators' own Glory Boy had been on recon for the past twenty five years, training and preparing for this exact moment in history. From his start, Coach Spurrier transformed the Florida Gators into a national football powerhouse. The decades-long drought of conference championships was immediately over. Whereas we had a dearth of championships for six decades, Spurrier flooded the fan base with conference championships. The 90's became the Decade of the Gators with Southeastern Conference Championships in 1991, 1993, 1994, 1995, 1996, and 2000.

Coach Spurrier brought excitement back to "The Swamp" – the new label he coined for Florida Field. The Gators' high-scoring *fun 'n gun* offense and bone-crushing defense, combined with an ear-shattering home field fan base lead to a record string of home victories. The Swamp became hallowed ground where "only Gators get out alive."

Gator Fans at The Swamp

The Miracle

Coach Spurrier had made possible what many had resigned themselves to as impossible. He not only won a conference championship, he won six in a single decade! What eluded the Gators for sixty years, he quickly made up for. For an entire decade, the Gators dominated the Southeastern Conference. But, once the Gators had the satisfying taste of victory in their mouth and the confidence they could take on anyone, the Head Ball Coach pulled off the ultimate miracle in 1996...

One of the great traditions in college football are the rivalries – the absolute hatred between certain schools. I mean these rivals are so strong that families sometimes split over it – like Romeo and Juliet's Capulets versus the Montagues or Andy Griffith's Hatfields versus the McCoys. These feuds go back generations. They're blood deep.

For the Gators, our arch-rivals are the Georgia Bulldogs and the Florida State Seminoles. The rivalry with the Bulldogs goes back to 1915. The game's played every year in Jacksonville, Florida (a neutral field) and has come to be known as the "world's largest cocktail party." It's true. The one time I took Mom there a few years ago, a student in the row behind us dumped his beer down Mom's back.

It's a bitter rivalry. In fact, it was the loss to Georgia in 1966 – the year of Steve Spurrier's Heisman – which dashed Florida's hopes for its first conference championship that year.

Georgia has won fifteen conference championships, including 1966, and two national championships. They've fielded two Heisman Trophy winners. They're tough. Gator fans love to hate Georgia and their ugly bulldog mascot, Uga. And the feelings are mutual on the other side.

One Ugly Mascot, University of Georgia's Uga

And then there's the Seminoles – from the Girl's School at FSU (Florida State University). It's called the Girl's School in reference to the fact that the university was all women until 1947 when it shifted to co-ed and a football team was fielded. It's Mom's alma mater (remember the Romeo and Juliet reference) where she was a sorority sister with Faye Dunaway. Burt Reynolds played football at FSU, where he roomed with Lee Corso of ESPN College Gameday fame.

"Girl's School" is a derogatory term referencing the lack of the respect for FSU's football program – which was historically bad (worse than the Gators). However, that all changed in 1976 with the hiring of Coach Bobby Bowden. Coach Bowden did the impossible and transformed the Girl's School into a football powerhouse which won three national championships and fielded three Heisman Trophy winners (same as University of Florida today). Whereas, in the old days, the FSU game on Florida's schedule was an automatic win, that changed with Coach Bowden. So, between Georgia and FSU each year, Gator fans could always anticipate a battle. In 1996, the battles with these two rivals would be epic – battles for world domination (at least in the college football world).

That year, the Gators started the season ranked as the 4th best team in the country. As always, their schedule included both Georgia and FSU as the two main rivalry games. The Georgia game was first, in its traditional early November slot. The Gators came into the game undefeated and, unfortunately for Georgia, Coach Spurrier has a great memory and held a thirty-year grudge over his own bitter loss to Georgia back in 1966. The Head Ball Coach got even for Georgia's transgressions of three decades prior when the Gators routed Georgia 47-7! Gator Nation was ecstatic.

The Gators were still undefeated going into their final regular game of the season to take on FSU at their home field in Tallahassee. The Gators were ranked #1 nationally and now had their sights on a national championship bowl game. Their clean-cut loveable quarterback, Danny Wuerffel, was a leading Heisman Trophy candidate – just like Steve Spurrier had been thirty years prior. You couldn't script an opera any better than this show-down. All the Gators had to do was get past Bobby Bowden's Seminole team. Just one problem...

The Seminoles were likewise undefeated and ranked as the second best team in the land – likewise fighting for a spot in the national championship game. The matchup was called the "Game of the Century" and rightfully so. It pitted two teams who in prior decades were not even taken seriously in football circles; the idea of national championship play would have drawn laughs. No laughing anymore – both teams were formidable. Downright tough (especially for a Girls School).

Gator Nation had their hopes and dreams up going into Tallahassee. Prayers ascended yet again into the heavens for the victory which would assure the Gators of a national championship bowl spot to play for all the marbles. Yet, despite the prayers, it seemed God didn't have time for the Gators that Saturday. The

Gators lost 24-21, seemingly knocking them out of consideration for the national championship. Gator Nation was devastated.

Coach Spurrier complained that the Seminoles made late hits against Quarterback Wuerffel. He even produced video footage afterwards of a half-dozen late hits that were not flagged. Bobby Bowden responded that he thought the hits were clean while admitting that, "we just hit to the echo (of the whistle), instead of the whistle." That smart-aleck remark didn't sit well with Steve Spurrier or Gator Nation. Coach Spurrier tucked it away on his list of grudges.

With the regular season completed and with one loss, the Gators assumed their hopes for a national championship game were dashed. They played the SEC championship the following Saturday against Alabama who they soundly beat 45-30. The Gators secured their fifth conference championship and fourth in a row. An astounding year but seemingly at the expense of the national championship. It was hard to be excited with just a conference championship and an expected inconsequential bowl placement. But apparently God had been listening to the Gator Nation prayers bombarding heaven going into the fateful FSU game and he now found time to answer.

On that Saturday when Coach Spurrier and Florida swept by Alabama for its fifth SEC championship, there were additional championship games going on in the other conferences. It turns out that the outcome of those games would be the answer to the Gators' prayers. That same day, in the inaugural Big 12 Championship, Texas upset Nebraska, securing the Gators a spot in the Sugar Bowl on January 2, 1997 against FSU. There would be a rematch.

But then another miracle occurred, at the Rose Bowl game on New Year's Day 1997, Ohio State upset second-ranked Arizona State on the last play of the game. This upset victory on January 1 set up the January 2 Sugar Bowl rematch between arch-rivals Florida and FSU as the Bowl Alliance National Championship game. The Gators not only had a rematch with arch-rival FSU, but they would go mano-a-mano for the undisputed national championship! Shakespeare had nothing on the football drama being played out. God is a college football fan!

Following the loss in Tallahassee a few weeks earlier and Bobby Bowden's "echo" comments to Coach Spurrier, the Game of the Century Part Two saw a determined Gator squad and coaching staff – out for revenge and the university's first national championship; they would not be denied. Danny Wuerffel entered the game, having been selected as the Heisman Trophy winner for 1996. Coach Spurrier adjusted Danny Wuerffel's offense into a shotgun formation to give him more time in the pocket to avoid the late-hitting Seminoles and Wuerffel used that time to pick apart the Seminoles defense. The Gators routed their arch-rival Seminoles on the absolute last game of the season to the score of 52-20 and the Gators secured their first national championship! A national championship won handedly against arch-rival FSU; coached by a Heisman Trophy Gator; and won by a Heisman Trophy Gator. *As It Should Be*!

Three Wise Men

That 1996 National Championship was the apex of Steve Spurrier's coaching career at Gainesville and he forever changed Gator football into a national powerhouse. His teams were always competitive and The Swamp became known as one of the most hostile away-games any team could schedule – thanks to the rabid Gator fans. Coach Spurrier set the bar for Gator football that exists today – nothing but a national championship is acceptable. And when the Head Ball Coach (mistakenly) left Florida in 2001 to coach the professional Washington Redskins, the next stewards of the brand were expected to continue the tradition he established. Any head coach who couldn't deliver was simply moved out - quickly. Gator Nation demanded championships – the national kind.

In 2005, Urban Meyer took over the Gators football program as its head coach following a lackluster performance by his predecessor. He immediately returned the Gators to greatness and delivered not one but two more national championships in 2006 and 2008 - #2 and #3! And he did it with the Gators' third Heisman Trophy quarterback, Tim Tebow (or Timmy as my wife calls him).

Cut from the same clean-cut Christian mold as Danny Wuerffel, Tebow leveraged social media – a phenomenon that did not exist in Wuerffel's time - to become America's darling. Within less than two decades of Steve Spurrier's return to The Swamp, the Gators went from zero conference and national championships to eight conference championships and three national titles. And added two more Heisman Trophy quarterbacks.

Today, those three wise men (Spurrier, Wuerffel, and Tebow) are enshrined for immortality as statues outside the Football Holy Land of newly renamed "Steve Spurrier - Florida Field" - awaiting the next Gator Heisman to join them along with the next national title(s).

Three Heisman Wise Men at Florida Field
(Tim Tebow, Steve Spurrier, Danny Wuerffel)

It's Religious But No Kneeling Here

I've pointed out the religious-like traditions that draw fans of all ages back to college football games. Prior to moving back to Florida, Kim and I went so far as to travel each weekend from Texas to Florida for two years just to attend the Gators' home games. We did it to relive the excitement, enjoy the traditions, and reconnect with lifelong friends.

During those two years, we tailgated and/or otherwise reconnected with our Lakeland people: Paul Templin, Eric Templin, Jana Finnan, Diane Moore Muldoon and her husband, Tim, Annette Armstrong Johnston and her husband Ken, Chris Sikes and her son, Jamie Sikes. We're all middle-aged now but the traditions draw us back. It's a return, if not to our actual alma mater (Kim is an alum), then at least our spiritual one.

Gator Tailgating with Lifelong Friends, 2018.
Lance, Annette Johnston Armstrong & Husband, Eric Templin
and Jana Finnan, Paul Templin

We live in a time of change – increasing ever more rapidly because anyone with an Internet connection gets to voice their opinion and make noise on every conceivable topic under the sun. Our traditions and mores are being assaulted as a result of the ease of global opining. In a world of increasing noise, it's even more important to honor and practice our traditions, which keep us centered.

The same things that were done at Gator Games in 1966 are being done today: Opening march by the Fighting Gator Band, the National Anthem, the Pledge of Allegiance, the fly-overs, Mr. Two-Bits, Homecoming Gator Growls, and tailgating. With these time-tested traditions, we can draw confidence that all is and will be well, amidst the presence of post-9/11 marksmen guarding each entrance to Steve Spurrier-Florida Field. Following and exercising these traditions symbolize and represent our collective respect for all things great, including our military.

When the National Anthem plays at the start of a Gator Game, no one needs to be told to stand. We stand. No one needs to be told to remove their hat. We remove our hats. We place our right hand over our heart as we were taught in kindergarten. We sing the words. We applaud the flyover. And we don't need to point out to ANYONE that there's no kneeling allowed. It's not even considered. Frankly, I've always imagined that if a person anywhere were to dare to take a knee, he'd need help getting back up; there'd be a pile-on. That's just how strong the feelings run in Old Florida – thanks to our traditions. And thanks to college football.

We Are the Boys of Old Florida

One of the traditions at Florida football games which has existed since the 1930's is the singing of the alma mater, "We Are the Boys of Old Florida." It's sung each game during the break between the third and fourth quarters. Everyone stands, puts an arm around the person to either side of them and sings the words in unison, while swaying back and forth in concert. Ninety thousand fans participate.

What's not widely known is that the same melody and very similar lyrics have been used for as long at other schools, such as the University of Nebraska, the University of Chicago, and the Toledo, Ohio public school system. For example, compare the lyrics in the respective alma maters for Florida and Nebraska...

Florida Alma Mater	Nebraska Alma Mater
We are the boys from old Florida, *F-L-O-R-I-D-A.* *Where the girls are the fairest,* *The boys are the squarest ...* *Of any old state down our way.*	*There is no place like Nebraska,* *Dear old Nebraska U.* *Where the girls are the fairest,* *The boys are the squarest...* *Of any old school that I knew.*
We are all strong for old Florida *Down where the old Gators play.* *In all kinds of weather ...* *We'll all stick together...* *For F-L-O-R-I-D-A*	*There is no place like Nebraska* *Where they're all true blue.* *We'll all stick together...* *In all kinds of weather...* *For dear old Nebraska U*

Notice the similarity? Of course, all the other schools copied the University of Florida. (At least that's the version I'm going with.)

Dad's Last Game

In June 2000, Dad received his cancer diagnosis. Terminal. Six months, maybe. He was sixty years old.

I was living and working in Houston and, with his prognosis, I made frequent trips to Florida to spend final time with him. When Fall approached, what we really had together, including all of his friends, was college football and the Gators. We could all gather around the old Zenith TV in his living room and hoot and holler over our beloved Gators. Dad would have side bets going and it was just like old times. I hope it helped, at least temporarily, to take his mind off his pending exit.

Uncle David had season tickets to the Gator games and he made a set available to me so Dad, my ten-year old daughter, Stephanie, and I could go watch a game at The Swamp. It was Stephanie's first live Gator game; Dad's last.

It was early in the season so the Gators were playing some push-over team like the Nuns of Sister Teresa. It was a typical tune-up game where the Gators get to overpower some smaller school and the smaller school receives a check for a half-million bucks or more.

Nevertheless, the fans were rowdy and all the traditions were there. It had been a good twenty five years since Dad had last taken me to a Gator game when I was just a teenager.

We got to scream at the touchdowns, curse the fumbles, yell "Go Gators" in harmony with the band, and sing "We Are the Boys of Old Florida" during the third quarter break. It was a fun time albeit sad knowing this was the last one for him. On the two-and-half hour drive home to Lakeland that evening, Dad told me his old stories as we passed familiar places. He told me about catching shell crackers (that's a fish) in Lake Panasoffkee; he told me about his crazy citrus buyer, Harold Collins - random discussions which flowed from his stream of consciousness at the time. I always wonder what I'll recall and think about when I'm presented with the same situation as Dad.

Our mutual love of the Gators and college football allowed us to enjoy that last Fall together. Today, those same seats where Dad, Stephanie and I sat in 2000 are where Kim and I sit for each home game - in the North end zone. And every time I make my way to them, I think of that final Gator game with Dad. *As It Should Be.*

Kim and Lance at a Gator Game - in Dad's Seat, 2016

The Back Story

For additional background information, audio and video interviews and/or the unpublished photos for this chapter, visit:

BONUS: The Back Story – This is Gator Country
http://www.AISBbook.com/Ch08

Chapter 9

The Code

In 1996, I was faced with a dilemma that changed everything for me...

I was ten years into my career with the company I joined straight out of college, Setpoint. And my career was on the rise. I had made a good reputation for myself as an engineer and manager who could get the difficult jobs done while delivering strong profits back to the company. I was confident for the future. Along with our five-year-old daughter (Stephanie), Eri and I had just built and moved into a new home in Houston that was a financial stretch for me; I made the leap based on my confidence in my corporate future and because I wanted the best for them. When I went into work on Monday, January 8, 1996, everything looked rosy for me and my young family.

Within the first hour of work, I was called to a manager's meeting to learn that Setpoint was being acquired by a company called Aspen Technology (AspenTech). This was not too earth-shattering in that AspenTech was a strategic partner to Setpoint and in fact, I was heavily involved in the success of that alliance, going after a common competitor, Dynamic Matrix Control Corporation (DMCC). Over the past eighteen months, the Setpoint / AspenTech alliance had continually nudged DMCC from its premier niche spot and won away project after project. So the news was interesting and not totally unexpected. Then the second shoe was dropped...

That past Friday, AspenTech had also secretly acquired DMCC! AspenTech had acquired the two top players to effectively establish what would be considered a monopoly if not for the fact that our business was such a small niche arena. By the next afternoon, I found myself (along with every other Setpoint manager) in the large conference room at arch-rival DMCC's Houston office with the DMCC managers and AspenTech executive team. We were effectively being told, "Welcome to the family. You boys now need to learn to play together." You might as well have put the Gators and Seminoles football teams in the same room and tried telling them the same. There were hard feelings all around. And total uncertainty over the future.

What proceeded over the next year was a classic culture clash in trying to merge the three companies. You had the Setpoint culture of an Inc500 engineering company with systems and processes, run by professional project managers; the DMCC good 'ole boy engineering organization that did not believe in project managers – it was run like a small family business. And finally, you had the aggressive sales-driven culture of AspenTech – single-mindedly focused on doing whatever it took to keep their NASDAQ stock price up. Almost overnight, my rosy future was up for grabs as everyone in Setpoint and DMCC jockeyed for a seat at the table; power and position was immediately at stake. It was a cage match. And AspenTech was not prepared – or equipped - for the culture clash.

Early in the process, I was invited to dinner by one of AspenTech's executives (Earl) who knew me from my contributions to the successful Setpoint / AspenTech alliance – whose success was a precursor to the AspenTech double coup of DMCC and Setpoint. Over dinner, he was promising me the moon (a promotion, a salary increase, stock options) - reassuring me not to be concerned of my position in the new combined organization. He had big plans for me; on one condition...

He didn't like my boss - my senior mentor for the past five years, John. John had done for me, my career and my young family's financial security more than any man living. He had coached me, taught me, sponsored me and created new assignments just for me during my rise at Setpoint. John always had my back. You look back over your life to identify those handful of people who really made a difference in your career. Well, John was one of them.

Earl and John had never gotten along during the alliance days – there was a basic business philosophy mismatch and outright mistrust. And, as a result, it was this AspenTech executive's intent to run John out. He casually spelled it all out to me over fajitas. While Earl outlined the plan to oust my most trusted mentor, he simultaneously painted the rosy picture of my future as long as… you guessed it. He specifically told me that I could not divulge his plans to John.

I was shocked. And pissed. How dare this guy play Machiavellian games with me, my mentor and my family. He had basically laid it out there with this proposition: "Lance, you can keep quiet, play along while I boot out John and you'll ride AspenTech's wave to financial gain. Or you can share my plan to John; at which point, your career at Aspen is basically over."

As dinner was finished, I thanked him for dinner and drove home – rolling the problem over and over in my head of what to do. I was faced with the dilemma of protecting my family's financial security by allowing my most trusted mentor to be taken down or I could protect John and put my family at financial risk with my career weakened. The moment I got home, the first person I called was Dad.

I spelled it all out for Dad: the change of fortune, the cage match culture, the dinner, the conversation, the overt threat. I started to wrap up by saying, "Dad, this guy asked me to betray my mentor…" Before I could finish the sentence, Dad had heard all he needed to hear and he abruptly cut me off, saying, *"We don't do that."* Followed by silence. There endeth the lesson.

He was right. And it was that simple. In that one sentence, Dad reminded me to follow The Code, the same code that had been taught me growing up in Old Florida: *to respect men, our traditions and the land.* We don't betray our loyalties – no matter the costs. In a nanosecond, it became crystal clear what I needed to do.

I hung up with Dad and immediately called my mentor, "John, I know it's late but I need to talk to you about something." I shared my entire dinner conversation and the plans against him. He thanked me, told me not to worry and he'd see me in the morning. I had done the right thing – it was one of those simple decisions. I had sustained my loyalty but now I'd have to be prepared to fight like hell for myself (and my family) at AspenTech. I had just created an enemy with a powerful person at Aspen.

I've faced similar decisions throughout my corporate and entrepreneurial career and I've discovered that the decision is always simple, but often painful. However, I've also discovered that if you follow The Code, the universe miraculously conspires to protect you. The balance of justice is maintained. In this case, Earl – the senior AspenTech manager who threatened my career if I didn't betray a loyalty - didn't last long enough with the company to see any of his plans through.

And as for the fate of John, my most trusted mentor, he was still at AspenTech when I retired ten years later – a very respected member of the senior management team. And last man standing. *As It Should Be.*

Lesson (re)learned: Follow The Code.

What Is The Code?

The Code is certainly not limited to Old Florida, nor any region, nor any country for that matter. In fact, when I was courting Eri in Japan, I discovered the Japanese have a name for it: bushido - the way of the samurai. In Florida, we don't have a name for it; I simply call it "The Code." But if you'd quiz a dozen adults who grew up with me on how to act in certain situations, they'd each give the same answer, drawn from The Code, as passed down to them.

Dad's phrase, *"As It Should Be,"* was his response, his acknowledgment, to any act or event which was in accordance with The Code. And like I said, it's certainly not limited to Old Florida. Over the years, I've found the phrase naturally resonates with so many people from different backgrounds. It's simply a code phrase to a way of life; a philosophy. And hopefully, if I've done my job adequately, you can now see these Old Florida tales and vignettes in the whole context of *As It Should Be.*

The Code is unwritten and derived from - what some would say today are old-fashioned chivalrous traditions but what those of us of Old Florida stock would defend as not old-fashioned but rather time-tested. How can traditions be old-fashioned? Frankly, what we need more of is respect for and practice of the traditions. The traditions keeps us centered as a society.

The Code's foundation is the wisdom that there is a natural order to things. This natural order is a delicate balance, with fragile connections. Failure to respect the balance and to acknowledge the connections leads to "unintended consequences" as Stephanie learned at college and I learned from her. This is not some metaphysical voodoo. It's serious stuff. Recall the Butterfly Theory of Chaos I introduced in Chapter 3 – the principle that a butterfly fluttering its wings in China can lead to a hurricane in Florida.

As Exhibit A, look at what happened in my corporate AspenTech story amidst the threats to me and my mentor, John. I maintained my loyalty. I followed The Code. I was left standing. As was John. Others who didn't follow The Code, well… they didn't fare so well. In fact, once things calmed down at Aspen and we all learned to get along, I prospered for the next decade – without having to betray a single loyalty.

The Code was developed and lived by our ancestors to protect the delicate balance of the natural order. Through experience, they recognized the causality of interfering with these fragile connections and The Code has been passed down generation to generation as accumulated wisdom. That's why we study history; to identify the connections with the benefit of time and a rear view mirror.

Just as I learned from growing up around my family and their friends, The Code is grounded in a single word: respect; *respect for men, respect for the traditions and respect for the land.* Violate any one of those connections and the delicate balance is lost, like a tight rope walker who missteps. Now what does all that really mean? How is The Code reflected in our lives?

Well, you don't need anything as dramatic as my corporate dilemma to live or witness The Code. It's captured in the small everyday moments of conducting our lives. For example, in Florida and the Old South, we say "Yes ma'am" and "Yes sir" to anyone no matter their age or financial station in life. It's respect. It's politeness. When I was growing up, if a five-year-old boy or girl failed to use those phrases, they were quickly corrected by their parents, "Yes, what…?"

"Yes ma'am" or "Yes sir" was the retort until it became ingrained in the deep well of their subconscious.

As a young gentleman, we are taught to open the door for a lady. When on an elevator, the gentleman allows the lady to enter and exit first. It derives from the tradition of the male protecting the female. When a man escorts a lady on a sidewalk where there's traffic, he positions himself between the lady and the traffic – like a shield, the symbol of the male. Again, respect for the sexes.

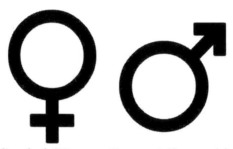

Female Symbol (Venus - Bronze Mirror with Handle)
and Male Symbol (Mars - Shield & Spear)

It also means that when a man sits in a restaurant, he never accepts a seat with his back to the door. He selects the seat with his back to the *wall* so that he can see and be prepared for any threat. Each of these are chivalrous practices which are derived from The Code. It's our heritage.

None of these practices take anything away from equality amongst the sexes. The practice by men is accepted by powerful women who acknowledge the natural order established within The Code. I've never heard a complaint or had a refusal from any woman when I practiced the above – whether family member or stranger, young or old.

Respect is further reflected in The Code's expectations of loyalty, courage and honor. It's why we revere the military and the honor of serving. It's why we love college football and the traditions that extoll these virtues - as in the public community display of respecting the flag and the honor of a standing ovation afforded our veterans and active military at each Florida football game. It's why our Old South feelings about protecting confederate symbols are so strong – these are all long-established symbols of loyalty, honor and courage; symbols of The Code.

The Code is also reflected in justice, character and self-control. The mother who draws a pistol from her purse to shoot dead the man endangering her and her baby is cheered. That's justice. The Marine, now civilian, who stops a hold-up in a convenience store using just his bare hands and his courage; that's character. That's justice. That's applauded. That's The Code, in action.

Those acts are each examples of demonstrating respect for men and respect for the traditions. But what I haven't covered yet is respect for the land. In the next chapter, I'll point out the unintended consequences of not respecting the land. What happens when we tip the delicate balance with the land, and the fragile connections become all too evident – as is occurring right now in Florida.

Mom

I've used lots of male examples of The Code but obviously men are not the only ones who follow it. It's lived by the fairer sex as well in Old Florida (and elsewhere). And no one lives it better than Judy Porter Edwards Hopkins, otherwise known to me as Mom.

Mom was the steady force, the silent power, the reliable one. Mom was always there for Brian and me. She made the sacrifices. She exemplified The Code to us.

The male is the sex whose symbol is the shield, representative of the stronger sex. Frankly, that's a nice symbology but my observation is that there is no one tougher than a mother. It was the case with my Eri and it was certainly the case with Mom. To hell with equality, women are stronger than men.

Mom has kicked cancer's butt three times. She did it with silent courage. Whenever the diagnosis came, Mom jumped on the regimen immediately, "The sooner I get started, the sooner I'll get it beat." A dainty woman, I can imagine her on the Florida frontier one hundred seventy years ago with my 4X great-grandfather, James Alderman, crossing the Alafia River and telling them all to hurry it up. She's that tough; silent tough.

About fifteen years ago, Mom had a health scare where a reoccurrence of cancer was on everyone's mind. I got the call in Houston and I immediately flew to her in the hospital in Lakeland. After four days of hospital tests, she was in pain and vomiting and her surgeon, Dr. Thigpen, had run out of options. He ordered emergency surgery in the next two hours; to go inside and assess the problem. I put out the call, alerting family and close friends to Mom's situation. The response was akin to a muster call of our Old Florida ancestor, Timothy Alderman's Confederate Florida Regiment. Everyone answered and began arriving in masse, physically and online; ready for battle.

Brian was in route back from a Glades trip. Right before they wheeled Mom in to surgery, I caught Dr. Thigpen in the hall and explained how all eyes were on him as the reinforcements were on the way, with high expectations. I explained how Brian was actually driving straight back from Chokoloskee. "Did he catch any Snook," the doc asked. I replied, "Yes, he did as a matter of fact. And if you get Mom well, there's some Snook in this for you." The doc grinned and like the professional he was, he went inside, found NO cancer (thank God), and cleared a simple plumbing problem.

Before, during and after the scare, Mom was always cheerful – more worried about us than herself. She never shows her fear. Total courage, just like The Code says. Drawn from her Cracker spirit and blood.

Mom was the one who introduced me to Scouting. And, to my mind, there is no organization that teaches The Code better than the Boy Scouts. It's embellished in the Scout Oath and the Scout Law:

The Code

Scout Oath

*I will do my best to do my duty to God and my country
and to obey the Scout Law;
To help other people at all times;
to keep myself physically strong, mentally awake
and morally straight.*

Scout Law

*A scout is trustworthy, loyal, helpful,
friendly, courteous, kind, obedient, cheerful, thrifty,
brave, clean, and reverent.*

But, not only did Mom introduce me to Scouts – specifically entry level Cub Scouts – but in classic Mom fashion, she volunteered to create the den of my friends and be our den mother. She simply took the bull by the horns and taught us the beginnings of The Code.

Mom paid the dues for me and Brian. She never faltered, no matter the hardship - not once in my fifty seven years. She was the volunteer, the provider. She drove me to college in my old '68 Cougar and she cried as I dropped her off at the airport, symbolizing the end of one journey and the start of the next to find my own way. When Eri died, she was there for me immediately.

I've mentioned in a prior chapter that a signature moment in my life was my Eagle Scout award. The entire family turned out for it but two people stood out as having inspired me to achieve it: Grandpa Edwards and Mom. Mom got me started in scouting at age seven, she saw me thru it, she equipped me, she drove us, she helped me with my merit badges, and she was there on stage when it all culminated six years later. She gets all the credit. She put in the work. She always showed up for me.

Lance's Eagle Scout Ceremony, 1976
Mom Attaching the Eagle Medal

Mom made all the sacrifices for many years. And as the universe conspires to reward those who live The Code, she's rightfully so received her rewards. Mom and Dad divorced young but she remarried two great men, my stepfathers: Jeff Wiley, my late stepfather who died in 2002 and Duane Hopkins, who she married in 2007. A son couldn't ask for better men to look after his mother. Coincidentally, both men are retired Lieutenant Colonels. *As It Should Be.*

Today, Mom's healthy and going strong. When we're together, she's commonly mistaken for my wife thanks to her youthful appearance (and/or my aged one). As a cheerleader in high school, she's been my biggest cheer supporter. In 2002, when I was eyeing my options for leaving AspenTech and I launched my fledging side business, Mom was there for me - just as she was when she saw me start out as a cub in Scouting. As my first (free) employee, she conducted my first marketing campaigns; carefully and deliberately preparing, labeling, stamping, sealing and mailing five hundred letters per week to prospects.

Mom The Cheerleader (right)
Lakeland High School, 1957

Once the business was established and I wrote my first book, "How to Make Big Money in Small Apartments," she volunteered to edit it. Who better as an editor than a retired 15-year senior administrator to a Federal judge, charged with making sure legal writs and documents were absolutely correct! She caught every typo and error I missed. Her recommendations were always spot on. I suppose that's why it became a best-seller. And her fingerprints and suggestions can be found all throughout this manuscript. Any errors and omissions are mine.

But most importantly, Mom enjoys her life. She's circled the globe twice, has set foot on all seven continents and has visited every major league baseball park. She earned it. She's like the Eveready Bunny; she just keeps on going. She exemplifies The Code and the Florida Cracker spirit.

And, in 2018, when that fledging little company that Mom helped this cub launch in 2002 was recognized by Houston Business Journal as one the fastest growing companies in Houston, Texas for the fourth year in a row, I made sure she was there to celebrate with me. Just as with my Eagle award forty-two years prior. That's *As It Should Be!*

Houston's Fastest Growing Companies Ceremony, 2018
Lance and Mom (Judy Porter Edwards Hopkins)

Quiet Strength

You don't have to look too far to see who Mom modeled in learning how to live The Code: her mother. In Chapter 2, I introduced my maternal grandmother, Gladys Howze Porter, who I knew as Mama.

Mama was a child of Old Florida and the quiet strength of the Porter family. She was the reserved lady that you counted on, always. She was The Code. Descended from a Florida pioneer family, she was born a scant sixty years after her great-great-grandfather, James Alderman, became the first white man to cross the Alafia River into the Indian territory of unsettled Florida; just three years after Florida became a state.

She was born in 1910 and raised in Ft. Meade. And it would be just sixteen years later when she would marry my grandfather, Paul Porter, when he was twenty three. She actually dropped out of school to marry Papa, not an uncommon practice in 1920's Florida.

What was uncommon was to have motherhood cast upon her, overnight, at age sixteen when her own mother died giving birth to baby brother Ronald. Also orphaned was Mama's baby sister, eighteen-month old Janiece. Committed to her family and strong in responsibility, Mama agreed to raise Janiece. Mama's Aunt Alice agreed to raise Ronald.

Wow. In 1927, Mama, the sixteen-year-old newlywed, had to learn adult responsibility fast – with a new husband and an adopted daughter hitting her almost simultaneously. And, unbeknownst to her, there was a Depression on the way. She went thru the accelerated doctorate program of adult responsibility.

Mama (Gladys Howze Porter), 1970's

Mama grew up in the wild rural environment of Central Florida but she was the fine side of the Gladys Howze - Paul Porter merger. For seventeen years, she worked behind the counter at Gaines Jewelry Store in Lakeland where countless people knew "Mrs. Porter" as she helped them pick out a special gift for a loved one. She was a fabulous seamstress and made all the gowns for Mom and her two sisters; a skill she undoubtedly mastered during the Depression.

She was totally dedicated to her family. As a matter of fact, the reason she started working at Gaines was to earn extra money for Mom's college education; something she was committed to, despite the fact that neither she nor Papa finished high school.

Mama was the yin to Papa's yang. Papa was the fun gregarious persona I've described; my fun, care-free grandfather. Mama was the quiet, resolute, dependable anchor. They made a great team and interesting to watch. Here's an example…

When Mama was in her sixties and I was maybe ten years old, I took notice that Mama was the one who mowed their lawn, not Papa. She pushed an old, beat-up mower around their fairly large lot in the August heat. Well, after yet one more lap around that yard fighting the heat and sand spurs, she stopped in mid-mow, abandoned the mower in the middle of the lawn and declared to Papa, "Paul, if you want that yard mowed, you do it." Now, it was hard, if not impossible, to un-flap Papa so he simply replied, "Okay."

A couple days later, Papa came by our house and told Brian and me "Hop in the truck boys." He toted us over to his and Mama's house and took us into his work shed where, low-and-behold, there sat a brand-new, shiny-red *riding* lawn mower. "Hop on boys," he said. "Have fun riding around the yard. And try to drive in straight lines." Ha. He had solved that problem easy enough.

That solution didn't sit too well with Mama. After we had finished our joy-riding on the new mower that afternoon and had been deposited back to our home, Mama apparently laid down the law with Papa. She made it clear he was going to do the mowing. (I assume this because we were never invited back to ride the tractor.) Mama was a quiet lady but she could get riled up over some of the things that Papa would do. *As It Should Be.*

My Discovery

My journey has certainly led me to a far different place than I first imagined as a youngster growing up in Central Florida in the 60's and 70's. As I stated at the outset, this book is as much a philosophy as a history; a rear view mirror look over seven generations of my

Old Florida family and what got me here. And, more importantly, what are the fragile connections that reveal themselves from this backward look over time? I've shared some of those up to this point but there's one more discovery that may prove helpful. At least, I wish I had known it when I started. It took me decades of trial and error to figure it out. And my main discovery is this…

There are no rules. That's right. None.

There is a Code but really there are no rules beyond that. We are taught in school a set of rules for successful living but they are not exclusive, nor necessarily correct or right for everyone. At least, not anymore.

If we could break down the timeline of our lives, I realized a few years ago, that God allowing, there are four quarters to life, just like a college football game (Yes, really, more college football). The quarters are approximately twenty years each. And our lives are largely segmented as this:

1st Quarter: Learn the Rules
2nd Quarter: Discover the Rules are BS
3rd Quarter: Make Your Own Rules
4th Quarter: Cruise & Prepare for the Post-game

Now I say this somewhat tongue and cheek but it reflects my journey. I'm in the third quarter. I spent the first twenty or so years of my life learning the rules we are taught at school: Work hard, study hard and get good grades so you can get a good… job. I did that. Check that one.

Then I spent another twenty years in that good job, handcuffing my future and my family's financial security to a company with flawed managers - praying that I'd keep climbing that corporate ladder only to get more and more disappointed the higher I climbed. I clung to the rule that a good job means security. It was a painful lesson learning that was a crock as I watched the layoffs of friends, waiting when my time would come and I'd be put on the street to start all over again. That's what led to the current stage of my life, the third quarter.

Going into my third quarter, I had to defy forty years of formal education and employer conditioning. I effectively began my education all over – my real education - drawing on the rules of successful living from my Cracker grandfathers and ancestors. After all, they didn't attend college. It wasn't even an option for them. And yet, they enjoyed successful lives.

The third quarter is when I learned to embrace the fact that there are no rules to this thing. Our lives are a blank canvas and we are the artist. There's a million ways to go about it. If one doesn't work, try another. Or simply start over; like I did when I shucked the mirage of corporate job security for my own small business.

And that's why I'm now in the education business. Yes, I teach real estate investing but what I really teach is that the rules we were taught in school are not the only set and, frankly, they don't apply to everyone. So make your own rules. After all, this life we're blessed with is no dress rehearsal. We only get one shot at it so you might as well go for it. Don't worry, no one is looking. And, if they are, so what? It's your canvas.

Whereas I can speak of the first three quarters from experience, I've had to hypothesize the fourth chapter purely on observations of others. There's no guarantee we get a fourth quarter but it's my belief that if you've done the job right in the first three quarters – that is, you've followed The Code – you should be able to cruise in the fourth quarter; take your time to relax and enjoy the victory. And to prepare for the post-game interview.

Sunset Over the Florida Gulf. *As It Should Be.*

How I Made My Own Rules

If you'd like to know how I made my own rules and escaped from my twenty-year job, you can check out these free resources:

BONUS: How to Make Big Money in Small Apartments (book) FREE with S&H at http://www.AISBbook.com/FreeBook

BONUS: How to Make Big Money in Small Apartments (webinar) FREE at http://www.AISBbook.com/FreeWebinar

The Back Story

For additional background information, audio and video interviews and/or the unpublished photos for this chapter, visit:

BONUS: The Back Story – The Code
http://www.AISBbook.com/Ch09

As It Should Be

Chapter 10

Mother Nature Hikes Her Skirt

Originally I planned to end the book with the previous chapter on The Code, and preparing for your post-game interview. Instead, the horrid events of the Summer of 2018 outside my new home, while in the midst of writing this book, demanded the addition of a new final chapter. Those events further demonstrated that everything is connected. There is a natural order to things, be it nature or man; it's a delicate balance.

As the events unfolded and I posted on my Facebook page the photos of death I'll share here, I announced to family and friends that I was changing the final chapter of my book on Old Florida. A Facebook friend, Neil Garvey, aptly commented "I hope it's not the final chapter for Florida." How appropriate. And so, here in this added chapter, I make my final argument that everything is connected and Dad was indeed right when he said, "If you mess with Mother Nature, she'll hike her skirts and kick your butt." Well, she won Round 1.

2018 Wildlife Massacre

In June 2018, dead fish started washing ashore on all the beaches along Southwest Florida, including Palm Island. With the sun and decaying flesh, the stench quickly became unbearable. To combat it, the ferry operators were forced to adorn handkerchiefs over their nose and mouth like train robbers of the Old West. Locals recognized the scourge as red tide, indicated by the tingle in the back of your throat and automatic cough reflex each time you took a breath anywhere near the Gulf.

I introduced red tide back in Chapter 4 as a natural phenomenon I first learned about as a child at Nana's Anna Maria beach, in the 60's and 70's. Every few years, it would hit for a *couple of weeks*, leave some dead fish and then clear out; life would return to normal. Well, this phenomenon at Palm Island was certainly red tide but this one had been lingering around for *eight months* – punching again and again; it refused to clear out. (And even worse, unknown to anyone at the time, this was only the opening rounds. Mother Nature was carefully preparing to take her best shot yet; all in retaliation for Man breaking The Code concerning respect for the land.)

Continuing thru all of June and the following Summer months, Mother Nature kept on pounding. There was no reprieve from the bell. The dead fish didn't go away, the coughing and respiratory distress of us humans continued. And whereas red tide was notorious for taking out non-game fish like cat fish and pin fish, soon the beaches and passes were covered in our beloved Snook and redfish.

Then Boca Grande's little Boca Beacon newspaper started reporting one hundred pound tarpon and three hundred pound goliath grouper washing up on the beaches and floating dead in the pass. If this was red tide, this was unlike any that the old timers could recall. This was longer and more potent than ever.

Red Tide Fatalities – Summer 2018
Dead Snook

Late into the Summer season, as word spread about the death and stench on the beach, Summer beach-goers began cancelling their vacations and their fishing trips. An economic red tide started to creep ashore as local hotels, restaurants, shops and fish captains felt the effects of rapidly declining commerce.

The little Boca Beacon fell under criticism from local businesses for advertising the problem since the news was driving away business. And, for a while, sympathetic to the plight of their fellow small business owners, the small newspaper cut back on the bad news. That is, until Mother Nature changed the match from Queensbury Boxing Rules to an outright no holds-barred cage match. Everything up to now was only the warm-up. After decades of abuse, she was pissed. And she was seeking her revenge – with prejudice.

From June thru August 2018, there was a progression in the fish kills. It was a phenomenon that no one could remember. Each week, as Kim and I walked the beach to survey the carnage, the species of dead fish would change. It started with catfish and pinfish and then progressed to eels. (Frankly, having grown up in Florida, I didn't even know we had eels in the Gulf until I saw hundreds of them dead on the beach in front of our home.) The next week would bring a wave of horse shoe crabs. Another week would bring a wave of dead blue crabs. It was a repeated pattern of death; wave upon wave of progressive species: Fish Species A washed up on Week A, Species B washed up on Week B, etc. It was like a well-established plan; hauntingly like a plague.

But then the worst came. What no one had guessed or knew possible…

Too Close to Home

Old Timers have always said that the method by which red tide kills fish is it clogs their gills so that the fish strangle, while surrounded in a literal sea of oxygen. Hence, I've always been told you can eat fish that's crippled by red tide; the meat is unaffected. And, for that reason, non-gill breathing animals were historically unaffected by red tide. Well, Mother Nature had a special cocktail of red tide concocted for us and the other air-breathing wildlife.

Dead sea turtles started to wash up on the beach – in the middle of the turtle nesting season. Then porpoises. Never had porpoises, or any mammals, died from red tide. Then the lovable manatees started to perish. Our pod of five manatees in Rum Bay disappeared. (To this day, I hope they got away to cleaner waters but I don't know where that could have been.) By now red tide and its death stretched along the entire Southwestern coast of Florida from Ft. Myers in the South to Tampa in the North. Some fishermen followed the trail of dead fish miles out into the Gulf, beyond the beaches. Hundreds of dead sea turtles, porpoises and manatees were hauled out of the water.

Kim and I were on the front lines of the destruction. On the last day of August on a Friday evening inspection walk of the beach in front of our home, we came across this dead fella…

Red Tide Fatality - Summer 2018
Dead Sea Turtle In Front of Our Home

I cursed the situation out loud, far evident now that this was man-induced destruction (I'll present my case in a moment).

The next morning, I awoke and looked out upon the Gulf as I normally do – to take in the view. By now, after weeks of poisoning, the Gulf had transformed from its normal and beautiful green color to a coffee-like brown you'd find in the bottom of a sewer. As I looked out upon the sand bar, visible with the morning's low tide, I noticed something peculiar. "Oh no, it can't be," I thought. I ran upstairs to grab my binoculars and check it out. Oh no, it was. "Kim, come with me," I blurted out as I rushed down the steps.

When we got to the beach, I confirmed my worst fear. It was a porpoise, a large adult. Dead. He had floated up on our sand bar sometime in the night. This damn "red tide" had hit our backyard twice in twenty four hours – doing the impossible and killing air-breathing animals.

Red Tide Fatality – Summer 2018
Dead Porpoise In Front of Our Home

With this new corpse, my cursing on the beach was prolonged. We were now entering Month Twelve of what historically had always been a two-week red tide cycle. By now, the wildlife and economic destruction had caught the attention of the national press. The Associated Press even expressed interest in interviewing me about my porpoise photo, once posted on Facebook. However, my long-time Lakeland friend, Suzanne Harper Ebel, summed it up best when she commented on my Facebook - from Missouri: *"I am with you in spirit!!! These mammals are stronger than we are! If they can't withstand this toxicity, it's only a matter of time for us."*

By this time, I was shocked and pissed with the situation. Don't tell me this is just a natural phenomenon. Don't tell me that red tide has been around Florida for five hundred years and that all we have to do is stick our heads in the sand and the tooth fairy will make it all better. Don't tell me it's not man-induced.

Locals who were economically struggling from the shut-off in tourism began asking out loud, "Do you think we'll ever recover?" Or they'd ask me, "Lance, you're a real estate guy… what's going to happen to real estate values?"

After months of observing the carnage of my beloved Florida and the economic red tide ashore, and not hearing anyone (including the so-called experts) who could explain what was really going on, I decided to figure it out for myself. At least to try to make sense of it.

I'm no scientist but I am an engineer by training, accustomed to identifying and qualifying correlations and causal results. And I'm a human being with a moderate level of intelligence and common sense. It's often hard to realize what's going in when you're in the middle of a crisis but with the benefit of time and a rear view mirror, it's easy to identify the connections.

Hence, with the benefit of observation, hindsight and personal interviews of people who actually know what they're talking about, I'm making the case for how we are violating The Code and, in the process, killing Florida. You be the judge. And allow me to present my case, Your Honor…

An Algae By Any Other Name

First, let's start with two toxic organisms causing the death: red tide and blue-green algae.

I've already described red tide. It is a salt water algae bloom which has been a naturally occurring cycle along Florida's Gulf coast, reported for centuries. Red tide has been generally tagged as the cause of what I call the "2018 Wildlife Massacre," from Ft. Myers up to Tampa. (I'll come back to that.)

The even more toxic organism is blue-green algae. Whereas red tide does not actually turn the water red, blue-green algae is named for the green-colored inches-thick sludge that massively covers *fresh water* bodies affected by it.

Blue-green Algae; Stuart, Florida, 2018

So, let's recap the basics... Red tide grows in salt water. Blue-green algae thrives in freshwater and dies upon contact with salt water. But here's where the misunderstanding begins....

As an aside, there are a lot of scientists and experts with an opinion. Mostly their explanations go something like this, "Red tide is complicated. We don't know everything about it and more research is needed. Give us more money." How can you not know all there is to know about something that has reportedly been around for nearly five hundred years killing fish in Florida? You would think someone would have figured this out by now! Well, let me calm down and get back to the problem.

The first person I found who made any sense was a scientist named Garrett Stuart. Actually Kim found him. After months of wildlife killing off Palm Island, Garrett was invited to speak to a gathering on our island in October 2018. I was out of town and Kim attended. The minute I got home she told me about this man and what he said. What she relayed to me resonated as making sense. In fact, it supported my layman theories (which coincided with the views of other locals on Boca Grande) on what was happening. So I arranged to interview Garrett on my real estate podcast, Green Light REI.

Garrett's a hippie-cowboy who's not just a scientist, he is a trained *algae* scientist. He comes out of the agricultural industry where he worked on crop production in Kansas before moving to the Florida Keys where he saw the effects of our land and water mismanagement on the destruction of the Florida reef. Anyway, he's trained, passionate and has a real knack for making the complicated simple - unlike 99% of all scientists and engineers (Trust me. I know. *I are one*). He labeled himself Captain Planet and on his own dime, he made it his mission to educate the populace on the science behind what's happening to the state. In fact, if you'd like to hear the interview or read the transcript with Garrett, I've made it available to you for free.

BONUS: Lance's Interview on Red Tide with Garrett Stuart
http://www.AISBbook.com/Garrett

Back to the problem. Here's where the misunderstanding begins...

Blue-green algae is actually not an algae. It's a bacteria, called a cyanobacteria. You know "cyan-", like in cyanide but the "cyan-" root really is the Latin root for blue. This stuff is really bad. It affects humans and has been scientifically linked to Alzheimer's disease, Parkinson's disease and Lou Gehrig's disease. It's also linked to liver disease.

Blue-green algae (cyanobacteria) is found worldwide. In fact, if you really want to learn about this problem, watch the 2017 award-winning documentary Toxic Puzzle, narrated by Harrison Ford. It describes a multi-year research project on blue-green algae, in Guam, where the correlation was made between the cyanobacteria and human neurodegenerative disease. You can rent it on-line.

Blue-Green Algae Documentary, Toxic Puzzle

Each of these organisms is bad. But when combined, red tide and blue-green algae interact to make one super-toxic cocktail which led to the 2018 Wildlife Massacre. And it all originates from two massive screw-ups by Man:

1) We changed the hydrology, that is the plumbing, of Central and South Florida, and

2) We polluted our fresh water with algae-growing nutrients.

We Need a Plumber

To really understand Florida's problem (actually the nation's problem when you listen to Garrett), we have to go back nearly one hundred years to Florida's Lake Okeechobee. Lake Okeechobee is the largest lake in the state. It's huge. It's not the size of a Great Lake but its half the size of the State of Delaware, covering 730 square miles. Look at any map of Florida and you'll see it in the South. Besides being large, it's also shallow – averaging only nine feet (and less one hundred years ago).

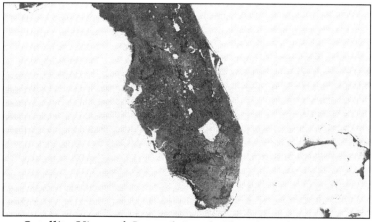

Satellite View of Central-South Florida Lake System
(Lake Okeechobee is the Largest Lake)

God designed Lake Okeechobee as part of Central and South Florida's entire water management system. Starting in Lake Kissimmee in Central Florida (recall my story with Papa Porter on Lake Kissimmee where he beached the boat), freshwater travelled South thru a flood plain of swamps and marshes to Lake O where it gathered in the giant basin. As the waters accumulated in Lake O, God allowed the spillover to filter down thru the "river of grass" of the Everglades, ultimately to Florida Bay and the Florida Keys to feed the Florida Reef (the third largest coral barrier reef in the world and the only one in the continental United States).

That's the original plumbing design which God intended. The Kissimmee – Okeechobee – Everglades ecosystem is a large single organism, designed to work in concert.

Starting at the turn of the 20th century, real estate developers and politicians saw that ecosystem as simply a swamp. And over the next few decades, federal and state-sponsored projects were conducted to drain massive portions of the Everglades, digging canals and building levees all across South Florida. God's Everglades wetlands in South Florida were converted to subdivisions and agricultural land, particularly sugar cane fields. The theme was to "tame nature" and "make the Everglades something useful, instead of worthless." This taming of nature and creation of new marketable real estate in South Florida sparked the Florida Land Boom of the 1920's.

However, the boom was short-lived. It crashed as the result of two devastating hurricanes which hit in 1926 and 1928. And those two hits by Mother Nature initiated the chain of events, which combined, led to the 2018 Wildlife Massacre – and all of the state's current water management problems. Let's look at the connections…

First, the 1926 hurricane hit Miami; catching the newly arrived pilgrims ill-prepared. They had mostly just arrived – each in pursuit of the Florida Land Boom. From Miami, the storm then whipped Northwest up the state to Lake O. With the lake churned up like an angry sea, the muck dike in the Southwest arc of the lake collapsed, flooding the town of Moore Haven and drowning as many as 300 souls.

In 1928, another hurricane hit Palm Beach, rolled West across the state and again flooded Lake Okeechobee. This time, at least 2,500 people were drowned from the floods when water poured over the simple earthen dike around the Southern perimeter of the lake.

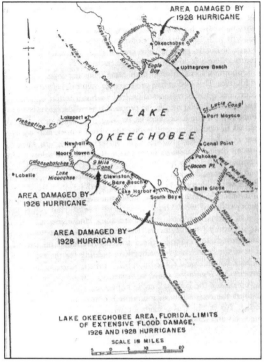

1926 & 1928 Lake Okeechobee Floods

Those two back-to-back catastrophes and the need to avert more flooding disasters brought about a bigger and better dike around Lake Okeechobee: the Herbert Hoover Dike, completed in 1937 by the Army Corp of Engineers. But we weren't done there.

Army Corps of Engineers Sign Advertising
Completion of Herbert Hoover Dike, 1937

To further protect Lake Okeechobee from breaching its new man-made banks, we changed its plumbing, adding two new drains to the massive reservoir. We took an ecosystem that used to naturally drain South, plugged up that drain and dug new drains East and West. Heading East, we dug canals to connect Lake Okeechobee to the St. Lucie River and Estuary near Stuart. And heading West, we dug canals to connect Lake O with the Caloosahatchee River where it discharges at Ft Myers. For the first time since Florida rose above the sea, Lake O now drained straight into the Atlantic and Gulf, bypassing the natural filtering system of the Everglades, installed by God.

But it doesn't even stop there. That's just the havoc inflicted on the ecosystem South of Lake O. North of Okeechobee, the low plains of Central Florida routinely flooded with heavy rains. So, canals and levees were likewise dug and installed there to tame nature and "drain the swamps." In fact, the long meandering Kissimmee River which originally travelled 93 miles to Lake O was actually straightened. That's right, we dug a 52 mile straight line canal to better control the water and provide more cattle land in Central Florida. The effect was a straight flow of unfiltered water from the Kissimmee cattle pastures into the Okeechobee reservoir, bypassing the natural vegetative filters of the original wetlands.

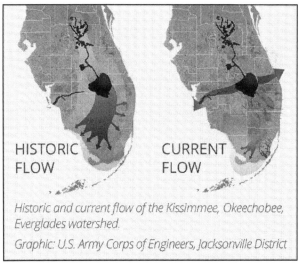

HISTORIC
FLOW

CURRENT
FLOW

Historic and current flow of the Kissimmee, Okeechobee, Everglades watershed.

Graphic: U.S. Army Corps of Engineers, Jacksonville District

Florida's Plumbing – God's Design vs. Man's Improvement

These were massive flood control projects performed by the Army Corps of Engineers over one-third of the state up thru the

1950's. As a kid, I grew up playing with Tonka trucks, moving dirt around in my backyard as a civil engineer would. These guys were playing with the real deal. The project was an engineer's dream; a proud piece of work. They even published a documentary on it, called Waters of Destiny. You can still see it.

BONUS: 1955 Waters of Destiny Video
http://www.AISBbook.com/WOD

In engineering, we talk about benefit-to-cost ratios, meaning if we invest $1 in a project, how many dollars come back? The Corps bragged their benefit-to-cost ratio for the flood control projects was 4:1. True. Impressive. Except we missed one little variable in that cost ratio, the "unintended consequences." There's that phrase again. Recall the Butterfly Theory of Chaos from Chapter 3.

When You Drain a Swamp...

The flooding problems of Central and South Florida were real. The land is at or below sea level and easily susceptible to flooding. However, the fatal flaw in the Corps' flood control projects was in not recognizing that the Kissimmee-Okeechobee-Everglades system is a single living ecosystem.

In fact, few did.

It wasn't until 1947 with Marjorie Stoneman Douglas' publication of *The Everglades: Rivers of Grass* that the world started to understand. Those three words, "rivers of grass," changed the understanding of the Glades as not a stand-alone swamp but rather a flowing river, starting from the Kissimmee Chain of Lakes. But by 1947, it was too late. The damage was done. We had taken a critical ecosystem in Florida and hacked it into pieces.

What were the effects?

First, with all of the levees and canals across Central and South Florida, water now came under the management of the federal Corps of Engineers (Corps), as it is today. When the growing population centers of Miami and Dade County demanded more water, the Corps would cut off the already dwindled flow to the

Glades from Lake O and route it to Dade. The Glades started to dry – and die. And in the process, so did the Florida Reef – that other ecosystem so critical for one-third of our sea life, which depends on the flow of fresh water from the Everglades system. (If the reef goes, we've got even bigger problems.) But that wasn't the only unintended consequence…

Hey Culligan Man!

If you've been around a few decades like me, you may recall the old TV commercials for the Culligan Water filter systems for your home. And the housewife screaming for help, "Hey Culligan Man!" A shout driven by the need to clean up the harsh water quality in her home. In fact, water quality has gotten so bad today that we actually buy bottled water (no more drinking from the garden hose like we did as kids… but that's for another book).

Well, with the straightening of the Kissimmee River, the building of straight canals, and the bypassing of the flow of water from Lake O, away from the Everglades' natural vegetative filters, we created a system that removed all of God's natural water filtration systems. With the straight canals, whatever went into the water in Kissimmee got a straight shot to Lake O and from there a straight shot to the Gulf and the Atlantic. Imagine running sewer lines straight into those bodies of water. That's what we have today and that was the unintended consequence of the flood control projects in the first half of the 20th century.

And that worked fine. For a while. Until the amount of pollutants in the water exceeded those body of waters' capacity to absorb them. And that leads to the second man-made reason for the 2018 Wildlife Massacre…

Garbage In = Garbage Out

Recall that the objective of "draining the swamps" was to convert wetlands into more profitable residential and agricultural use. Mission accomplished. But what comes with more residential and agricultural use of land? Answer: water pollution, specifically nutrients in the water.

Nutrients in the form of phosphorus and nitrogen, found in fertilizer run-off from farms, lawns, and animal and human excrement. Want to grow bigger tomatoes? Put fertilizer on it. Want to grow blue-green algae and red tide? Feed it fertilizer. And that's what we've done. We've assembled the world's largest system for channeling nutrients straight and unfiltered to Lake O to feed the cyanobacteria. Now, all you have to do is add heat and sunlight (which Florida has in abundance) and you've created the world's largest Petri dish for growing cyanobacteria.

When I was a kid, I had a fish aquarium. And if I didn't clean that water regularly, stuff would start to grow on the glass. Well, that's Lake O on a micro-scale.

When a cow poops in Orlando, that is connected to Lake O. When a septic tank leaks into the groundwater, that is connected to Lake O. When a sugar or citrus grower has fertilizer run-off from his fields into a stream, that is connected to Lake O. When we spray Roundup on our lawn and that runs off into the street and storm water with a good rain, that is connected to Lake O. There's nothing to stop or catch the nutrients flowing into the system. We've removed all the stops. Brilliant engineering. All unintended.

Nothing New

By the way, none of what I've reported is new or contested. It's been known for at least thirty years.

Native Floridian and country singer, John Anderson, famously sung about the state's plumbing problem and the draining of the Everglades in 1992. His song, Seminole Winds, accurately describes the draining of the land in search for "wealth untold" and in the "name of flood control." And, as a result... "the Glades are goin' dry."

When released, the song jumped to Number 2 on Billboard's Hot Country Singles. Just read the words in the lyrics...

Seminole Winds
by John Anderson, 1992

Ever since the days of old,
Men would search for **wealth untold**.
They'd dig for silver and for gold,
And leave the empty holes.
And way down south in the Everglades,
Where the black water rolls and the saw grass waves.
The eagles fly and the otters play,
In the land of the Seminole.

So blow, blow Seminole wind,
Blow like you're never gonna blow again.
I'm callin' to you like a long-lost friend,
But I know who you are.
And blow, blow from the **Okeechobee**,
All the way up to Micanopy.
Blow across the home of the Seminole,
The alligators and the gar.

Progress came and took its toll,
And in the name of **flood control**,
They made their plans and they drained the land,
Now the Glades are goin' dry.
And the last time I walked in the swamp,
I stood up on a Cypress stump,
I listened close and I heard the ghost,
Of Osceola cry.

So blow, blow Seminole wind,
Blow like you're never gonna blow again.
I'm callin' to you like a long-lost friend,
But I know who you are.
And blow, blow from the Okeechobee,
All the way up to Micanopy.
Blow across the home of the Seminole,
The alligators and the gar.

It's even better when you see and hear John sing it...

BONUS: Seminole Winds Video by John Anderson
http://www.AISBbook.com/John

With regards to our second problem of nutrient-infested water, the residents around the St. Lucie Estuary on the East Coast of Florida have been experiencing algal blooms since 1998 and as recently as 2016 before the 2018 Wildlife Massacre. Go online to YouTube and you can see the news coverage. You'll see the blue-green sludge clogging their waterways. They speak of the indescribable stench – a strange aroma of sewage and rotten eggs. Businesses closed. People suffering with breathing problems.

The problem with algae blooms is so well understood that a $7.8 billion Federal bill was passed to fix the problem, back in 2000! You know that if you can get those folks in Washington to agree on something then that tells you how well accepted the problem is. And how bad it is. But, I'm getting ahead of myself. I'll save solutions for a little later. We're only up to 2016 at this point.

So where are we so far? Well, let's summarize. Everyone agrees that 1) we have a plumbing problem and 2) we have a nutrients in the water problem. These two major problems combine to efficiently breed toxic blue-green algae in Lake O. A third and massive and serious problem just by itself. But how does red tide enter the picture?

Mother Nature is Pissed

Because we've understood the problem for decades and because we've taken little action on a solution voted into effect nearly twenty years ago, Mother Nature concluded we can't take a hint. And she'd run out of patience. So she sent a reminder back in October 2017. It was called Hurricane Irma. A nasty deadly hurricane that wreaked lots of property damage when she rolled up thru Central Florida (miraculously bypassing our home in Palm Island at the last minute). We thought Irma and the increased frequency of hurricanes was intended as yet another reminder from

Nature about the unintended consequences of global warming. Nope. Mother Nature had a bigger message in play.

When Irma hit Naples in Southwest Florida, she stumped the forecasters who predicted she would roll up the Gulf Coast with a fifteen-foot storm surge. Instead, she dodged right and went up the center of the state and straight over the top of Lake Okeechobee. To the absolute credit of the Corps of Engineers, the dike held. But Irma wasn't there to flood. She was there to churn up the Petri dish.

Her winds stirred up the shallow lake with its nutrient-laden muck bottom. Dormant nutrients which had been accumulating for decades were released as particulates into the water – left in suspension to wait for the warmth and sunlight of the next Florida Spring coming up in 2018. The Petri dish – the weapon - was locked and loaded. And that was the initiation of the final chain of events leading to the 2018 Wildlife Massacre.

Hurricane season in Florida runs each year from June 1 to November 30. Now, in practice the most active months are September and October. But in late May 2018, the Corps was monitoring the water level in Lake O, as they do each year heading into Hurricane Season. As stewards of the water, part of their responsibility is to maintain the level of Lake O such that it does not push the aging Herbert Hoover Dike beyond its capacity limits. If that dike were to give way in a hurricane and flood crowded South Florida today, the loss of life would dwarf what happened back in 1928.

The Corps manages the water level by opening up the locks that release water to the Gulf and Atlantic down the Caloosahatchee River at Ft. Myers and the St Lucie River in Stuart, respectively. So in May 2018, the water releases began, sending the coffee-brown nutrient-laden water to the larger bodies. The result was immediately observed. At Sanibel Island, near Ft. Myers, the Caloosahatchee discharge of coffee-brown nutrient-enriched sewage into the Gulf left a distinct demarcation line against the pristine green water of the Gulf.

Brown Lake O Discharge Hits the Green Gulf; June 3, 2018
Photo: City of Sanibel

Residents complained but the Corps was stuck between a rock and a hard place. They had to control the Lake O water level for public safety and a release to the East and West is the *only* degree of freedom they had. The nutrient-laden water kept coming and wouldn't stop for practically the entire hurricane season.

As we rolled into June and the temperatures increased, the Sun and warmth began to transform the coffee-brown water of Lake O, the Caloosahatchee River and St. Lucie Estuary into toxic blue-green algae. And the residents living and working around those discharge points gagged.

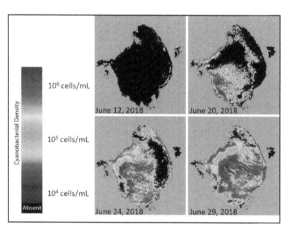

Explosive Cyanobacteria Growth in Lake O, June 2018 (NOAA)

Simultaneously, a red tide bloom had been hovering in the Gulf of Mexico since the time of Irma's run. Shifting winds would bring it back for a return hit along the Southwest Gulf coast every month or so. At the same time as the Caloosahatchee was serving as the breeding ground for blue-green algae in Ft. Myers, the red tide came in for another hit. And this is where, what I call, "Red Tide on Steroids" was created.

Red Tide on Steroids

Recall that blue-green algae can only live in freshwater; and red tide can only live in salt water. So when the blue-green algae coming down the Caloosahatchee River hit the salty Gulf, it died. Well, that was good news, and bad news. The good news was that it died. The bad news was that, upon death, it was back to another form of nutrient. And nutrients feed the red tide algae bloom. So, the deposit of blue-green algae nutrients into the Gulf served the same purpose as dumping fertilizer on your tomatoes. The red tide exploded.

And, as more and more nutrients were fed to the Gulf, the bloom intensified – moving up the state to Tampa and miles off-shore while, at the same time, becoming more potent. As the potency increased, a new species of sea life would land on our beaches – weeks and weeks of different waves of death.

Now, this next part is my *theory* as a layman, but I believe that at some point, the potency was so high that the algae actually mutated into what I call "Red Tide on Steroids." Whether it actually mutated or not, the concentration of toxins became so extreme in the Gulf that it started killing sea turtles, manatees and porpoises. And all during this hell, the Corps kept releasing more and more blue-green algae from Lake O and down the Caloosahatchee into the Gulf - because they had to. They were forced to keep pouring kerosene on the fire, feeding the raging inferno on our end.

But here's the clincher for me on my Red Tide on Steroids theory...

All during that intense period of death along the beach - of fish, reptiles and mammals - not one buzzard showed up. Not one.

Normally, you would see dozens circling with just a single dead animal. We had thousands dead, covering all species, and with the scent of death that couldn't be missed. It was a buzzard smorgasbord. Yet, despite that, not one buzzard circled. On normal red tides, buzzards land and do the clean-up. Not this one. They wouldn't touch this buffet. Even they knew this was something out of the ordinary.

Over the decades, thanks to ignorance and greed, we have engineered a very efficient wildlife killing machine – using our own state as the weapon. And that's where we committed our most severe violation of The Code. We lost our respect for the land. Mother Nature is reminding us yet again. This time, with prejudice.

The Solution

We understand the problem. So what's the solution? It's simple:

1) Return the Kissimmee – Okeechobee - Everglades Ecosystem back to its original flow, and

2) Get the nutrients out of the water.

Okay, now that I've solved that problem, let's get something to eat.

Ha. The problem is decades in the making. Think of the solution like this... First, we have to replumb our entire house *as we live in it* (and while more people are moving into it). And, secondly, we need a Culligan Man to install water filters in *every* house in town. Oh, and did I mention we have to get the cooperation of politicians in *both* Tallahassee and Washington?

Sounds impossible, doesn't it? Yet, there's one unintended consequence that's playing into our favor for a solution...

This problem is big, real and close to home. It's no tree-hugging, bleeding-heart environmental issue of saving some obscure left-handed spotted toad. This is both an ecological and economic crisis, not only to Florida (but to the world when you include the Florida Reef). It affects people's pocket books and their kids' health. You get enough well-to-do people pissed off and they start throwing money at a problem. And throwing politicians out.

When I was a college freshman taking Economics 101 in 1980, the world was in the midst of an oil crisis. Prices were spiking and I recall the talk that we could run out of oil. The single thing I remember from that class is this: the professor said, with confidence, that we will never run out of oil. The free market system would not allow that to happen. The price of oil would increase to ensure a supply-demand balance.

Roll the clock forward forty years and you see it's true. Today the United States imports more oil than it did in 1980. In fact, we now export oil – thanks to free market economics. The same economic balance will intervene into our water management problem.

Left unchecked and repeated, the Red Tide of 2018 is going to become an economic red tide for not just Southwest and Southeast Florida but the entire state. The state's leading industry is tourism. You start losing that revenue and the ripple effects will be like Irma slamming across Okeechobee: lots of unintended consequences. Mere economic survival will dictate action toward a solution.

What's disappointing is that the solution has already been approved. Passed in 2000 on a bipartisan vote in Washington, the Comprehensive Everglades Restoration Project (CERP) was designed as a $7.8 Billion project to accomplish the two objectives identified above as the logical solution. There's been some progress but little. After all, it's nearly twenty years after its passing and things are getting worse. The problem is greed, politics and bureaucracy. The State points the finger at the Feds for water management by the Corps. The Feds point the finger at the State for not acquiring the land South of Lake O to resume the flow southward.

Then there's the profit-driven originators of the nutrients: agriculture, cattle, septic tanks, fertilizer companies – each committed to protecting their own financial interests and pointing the finger at the others as the major violators, like a circular firing squad where everyone dies. And with their deep pockets for lobbyists, they can sway and delay any political moves which would effect a solution that's already agreed and would cut into their profits. That's the horrific part.

But like I say, you can only strangle people financially so long before they fight back. And you damn sure can't endanger their kids very long before they go primeval on you. That's why I have hope. Things will get worse before they get better. The only concern is that at what point do we pass the Point of No Return?

Everything is Connected

I started the book out on the premise that everything is connected, in our lives and now as we see, in our environment. Just like that butterfly in China can cause a hurricane in Florida, we now see – with the benefit of hindsight and a rear view mirror – the connections between our acts. And the penalties for violating The Code.

I'm the eternal optimist. I do believe we ultimately get it right, it's just that it sometimes comes at a high cost. In my seminars on real estate investing, a common fear which people have is that they might make a mistake and that fear stops them from taking *any* action. I rebut that fear by explaining that I have a core belief, which is, "I've never made a mistake… But I have had some expensive lessons along the way." And, as long as we heed the lessons and are open to them and act from them, the future is always brighter. It's always worked for me.

So, not wanting to leave you in a Debbie Downer mood, I leave you with this… We've learned the lessons over our cherished Everglades. We have the solution. Don't worry, we'll figure it out. We always do. Economics 101 says so.

The Back Story

For additional background information, audio and video interviews and/or the unpublished photos for this chapter, visit:

BONUS: The Back Story – Mother Nature Hikes Her Skirt
http://www.AISBbook.com/Ch10

Epilogue

I started this book with the Everglades and interestingly ended with the Everglades, and its undoing – which was not the plan but rather a requirement dictated by events during my writing. I left our cherished Glades at the end with hope of a recovery.

What started out as a labor of love on a simple narrative of Old Florida, intended only for close friends and family, evolved into a much deeper process of discovery about my roots and the connections across the land, the people and the times; all which conspire to lead each of us to our own unique lives and macro situations today. I discovered more about my home land and my own Florida ancestors than I had ever imagined. Surprising to me, since that was not my original intent.

I shared the philosophy of life I was taught and learned thru the lens of my Old Florida ancestors. I highlighted the unwritten philosophy which I label The Code: *our respect for men, the traditions and the land* – a timeless code which knows no geographical boundaries. And the unintended consequences which inevitably come from violating it. Simple stuff but profoundly and powerfully true – at least for me.

It wasn't until the end of the book that I realized the parallels of my own Old Florida ancestors with that of the fictional MacIvey family of the Florida classic, *A Land Remembered*. In fact, some of the parallels are eerily close...

A Land Remembered

If you're not familiar with the Florida classic, *A Land Remembered*, written in 1984 by Patrick Smith, it is a best-selling historical novel which spans three generations of a fictional Florida Cracker family, the MacIvey's. The period spans 1858 to 1968 from Central Florida (Kissimmee) to South Florida (Miami).

From the sweat of their brow and personal courage, the MacIvey family utilize what they find in the scrub country of Central Florida to amass a fortune in citrus, cattle and real estate; with each generation standing on the shoulders of the prior one. They endure starvation, mosquitoes, outlaws, freezes and hurricanes; remarkable parallels with my Old Florida ancestors who arrived in Central Florida in 1848.

At the end of the book, greed distorts third-generation Sol MacIvey, culminating in the draining of the Everglades in South Florida, to be replaced with condos and sugar fields. Only at the end of his life in 1968 does Sol MacIvey realize the actual costs of what he's traded. Sound familiar?

Thirty five years ago, Patrick Smith wrote of greed and the Florida land and water management problem, and the cost. In the process, Smith also indirectly revealed The Code. I've carried that story ahead fifty years to today to reveal what happens.

Unfortunately, the problem of over-developing the land and violating The Code is not unique to Florida. James Michener wrote about it in his historical novels on Hawaii, Texas, Colorado and Alaska. It is an endless cycle.

My Story

As I wrap this up, I sit currently in what I assume is the third quarter of my life. Of course, unlike a football game of my favorite

Gators, none of us know how much time we have left on the clock. I do wonder where the time went but I feel young and believe I still have plenty of time left for lots of serious chunkin' for Snook around Palm Island, with Dad's favorite 52M23.

Regardless, I'm immensely proud of my Old Florida roots, even more so than when I began this project; I now know so much more about them. I'm blessed to have their blood coursing thru my veins, and their wisdom in my mind. I'm proud to have been able to document and share them.

During the course of writing this book, Mom completed her own private book which she gifted to me, Brian and Stephanie on Christmas Day 2018. Titled "Generations," she chronicled the story of our ancestors going back three generations on both the paternal and maternal sides of my family. It was her act of love.

She started her book with this quote, which I'll borrow and use to end mine...

We inherit from ancestors gifts so often taken for granted. Each of us contains within us this inheritance of soul. We are links between the ages, containing past and present expectations, sacred memories and future promise.
-- Edward Seller

Lance. Snook On. Sunset. Palm Island.
As It Should Be

As It Should Be

Glossary

As Aristotle said, "All learning begins with definitions." Use this glossary as your guide to the jargon of Old Florida. Each of these terms is explained in the book:

52M23: black-and-gold-colored sinking Mirrolure. Dad's personal favorite color combination for Snook. And mine.

Ain't: "isn't" for anyone South of the Mason Dixon Line.

Blue-green algae: soupy green-colored freshwater algae that is not only toxic to fish and mammals but has been proved to cause Alzheimer's, Lou Gehrig Disease and Parkinson's Disease in humans.

Caloosahatchee River: Gulf coast river in Southwest Florida which discharges at Ft. Myers and connects Lake Okeechobee with the Gulf via man-made canals.

Chickee: Seminole Indian thatched huts; also used in context of covered camping docks scattered through the Ten Thousand Islands.

Chokoloskee: (pronounced Chuk-a-lusk-ee) an Old Florida outpost island at the entrance to the Ten Thousand Islands in Southwest Florida.

Chunkin': the art of casting an artificial lure under the mangroves in the pursuit of Snook. "I was a chunkin' and a chunkin."

Cyanobacteria: see blue-green algae.

Dolphin: confused with porpoise. Flipper was a porpoise. A dolphin is an edible game fish, now sold in restaurants under the name Mahi Mahi. The shift to the name Mahi Mahi was done to boost dolphin demand for those who thought, "Ooooh, I don't want to eat Flipper."

Fixin' to: "preparing to" for anyone South of the Mason Dixon Line. "I'm fixin' to go fishing."

Gators: name of the University of Florida football team; one of the greatest college football teams of the past thirty years. The University of Florida plays some other sports too, I think.

Hammock: see Pine Island.

Lake Okeechobee: largest lake in Florida and the root of water's primary water management problems in South Florida. Currently a petri dish for growing blue-green algae.

Manatee: aka Sea Cow. A placid, loveable mammal from which original mermaid sightings were claimed by sixteenth century Spanish explorers. (Those poor sailors hadn't seen women for many, many months.)

Mangrove: tree unique to South Florida's semi-tropical climate. It grows along the edge of salt water and houses Snook.

Mirrolure: an artificial casting bait for Snook.

'Noles: University of Florida's arch-rival Florida State University Seminoles. They play some football too.

Pine Island: a cluster of pine trees on the Florida prairie. Also known as a hammock.

Porpoise: Flipper was a porpoise, not a dolphin (despite the fact that the Miami Dolphins football team's logo is of a porpoise).

Redfish: Florida gamefish also found in abundance outside of Florida. Great fish to catch and eat but still second to Snook.

Red tide: saltwater-based algae that blooms on Florida's southern Gulf Coast. Toxic to fish and also mammals in high concentrations. Causes respiratory problems for humans and who knows what else.

Robalo: fancy name for Snook. Although you can't buy Snook in supermarkets, you can buy Robalo; shipped in in from Central America.

Scrub: the Florida wild of hammocks and palmettos. "We went hunting in the Florida scrub."

Snook: greatest fish ever assembled. Religion to some Florida anglers, including the author.

Snooky-looking: waters that look likely to hold Snook, evidenced by moving saltwater around mangroves and docks.

'Specs / Speckled Perch: freshwater perch once abundant in Florida's lakes. In Georgia, it's known as Crappie.

Spoon: an artificial fishing lure that resembles the working end of the eating utensil.

St. Lucie River: Atlantic coast river which discharges at Stuart in Southeast Florida; connects Lake Okeechobee with the Atlantic Ocean via man-made canals.

Tarpon:　a great and large sports fish but inedible, which places Snook as the King of the Florida game fish for excitement and appetite.

Bonuses

Here is a summary of the bonus resources referenced in the book:

BONUS: The Back Story – All Chapters
http://www.AISBbook.com

BONUS: Lance's Interview on Red Tide with Garrett Stuart
http://www.AISBbook.com/Garrett

BONUS: 1955 Waters of Destiny Video
http://www.AISBbook.com/WOD

BONUS: Seminole Winds Video by John Anderson
http://www.AISBbook.com/John

Real Estate Resources by Lance A. Edwards:

How to Make Big Money in Small Apartments (book)
FREE at http://www.AISBbook.com/FreeBook

How to Make Big Money in Small Apartments (webinar)
FREE at http://www.AISBbook.com/FreeWebinar

Made in the USA
Columbia, SC
11 January 2023

75908205R00141